For my mum, my No.1 fan.

Ching-He Huang is an Emmy-nominated TV chef and cookbook author. Born in Taipei, Taiwan, she uses fresh, organic, ethically sourced ingredients to create modern dishes that fuse Chinese tradition with innovation while remaining accessible for home cooks. Her immensely popular series include the Cooking Channel's *Easy Chinese: San Francisco*, *Easy Chinese: New York & LA*, *Restaurant Redemption*, and *Ching's Amazing Asia*. She has also appeared on *The Today Show*, *The Rachael Ray Show*, and *Iron Chef America* on The Food Network.

Ching has written seven cookbooks: *Eat Clean: Wok Yourself to Health*, *Exploring China*, *Ching's Fast Food*, *Everyday Easy Chinese*, *Ching's Chinese Food in Minutes*, *Chinese Food Made Easy*, and *China Modern*. She is also the creator of The Lotus Wok—a wok with a dynamic nano-silica coating for high performance cooking. Ching divides her time between the UK, the US, and Asia.

STIR CRAZY

100 Deliciously Healthy
Stir-fry Recipes

Ching-He Huang

Photography by Tamin Jones

Kyle Books

Published in 2017 by Kyle Books
www.kylebooks.com

Distributed by National Book Network
4501 Forbes Blvd, Suite 200,
Lanham, MD 20706
Phone: (800) 462-6420
Fax: (800) 338-4550
customercare@nbnbooks.com

First published in Great Britain in 2017 by
Kyle Books, an imprint of Kyle Cathie Ltd

10 9 8 7 6 5 4 3 2 1

ISBN 978 1 909487 67 3

Editor: Judith Hannam
Editorial Assistant: Hannah Coughlin
Copy Editor: Barbara Dixon
Nutritionist: Cordelia Woodward
Designer: Caroline Clark
Photographer: Tamin Jones
Food Stylist: Aya Nishimura
Prop Stylist: Wei Tang
Production: Nic Jones and Gemma John

Library of Congress Control Number: 2017941792

Color reproduction by ALTA London
Printed and bound in China by C&C Offset
Printing Co., Ltd.

Hello!

Thanks so much for choosing *Stir Crazy*. I hope it will inspire you to pick up the wok and have some fun when it comes to those all-important mealtimes!

Stir Crazy is a collection of delicious stir-fry recipes that I designed with busy people like you in mind. They are for all occasions and simple enough for everyday healthy cooking at home, with nutrition, taste, affordability, and balance in mind.

I've written a handful of books on Chinese cookery and being a Chinese cookery expert I always get asked the same questions: "How do I make a really good stir-fry so the veggies are crisp and fresh and don't get all soggy?" "I make stir-fries at home all the time but it's so boring. What flavors can I try?" "What sauces can I make?" "What tips and tricks can you offer?"

If these are the questions plaguing your everyday kitchen/stir-fry needs, then this is the book for you. I demystify the art of making a good stir-fry and offer you tips on getting it right. Whether it's a saucy dish or a crispy dry-fry, or whether you are a vegetable or meat lover, a novice or an experienced cook, here is a varied and wide range of dishes that I hope will help you increase your stir-fry repertoire.

So let's get started...and happy wokking!

Love

Mastering the wok

Why stir-fry?

Stir-frying is quick and it's easy to start, but it is not always so easy to master. Learning what separates a good stir-fry from a great one takes time and the willingness to do a wok dance (see opposite)! It is all about the timing—knowing when to add what and how to get the best out of each ingredient.

Stir-frying can also be inexpensive, and by cooking on a concentrated heat with a small amount of oil you retain more of the nutrients, yet the heat helps to break down the fibers, making the food easy for you to digest and absorb the nutrients.

This way of cooking is fun, fast, and can be healthy too, depending on what type of dish you are making and what you are putting into it.

Why use a wok?

This 2,000-year-old magical cooking pot is a way of life all over Asia and is used for sautéing, braising, frying, and steaming. It can be a challenge cooking for family mealtimes and an express tool such as this clever vessel can be a lifesaver on busy days.

How do I go about choosing a wok?

If you are really into healthy eating, I would suggest a stainless steel wok. It can be seasoned with coatings of apple cider vinegar, each coating evaporated to give a clear, thin nonstick layer. However, stainless steel as a material sometimes has uneven heat spots and food can stick, plus it doesn't retain heat as well as carbon steel.

Most professional Chinese chefs use unseasoned carbon steel woks, but they need a lot of love and care or they rust. Nonstick varieties, however, are not ideal since the coating comes off with time. Some carbon steel woks have a flat, wide base more like a saucepan, which is not a traditional wok shape, so look for ones with deep sides (to allow you to toss the food) and a small center (to concentrate the heat). Traditional woks are round-bottomed but these require a wok ring set over your stove, which is another added piece of equipment and not ideal for the modern home, especially induction hobs, which many homes have now.

Aluminum woks are inexpensive but they can rust and warp and are not as good conductors or retainers of heat as carbon steel woks.

My grandmother used to cook on a cast-iron wok and they are the best, but they are extremely heavy and it can be difficult to toss the food or maneuver them away from the stove when the heat gets too hot.

Whatever wok you have, however, I always say it's best to use it and not waste it. When it's on its last legs and you need a replacement, please do seek out my Lotus wok. I designed it for people who want a better wok experience. It is inexpensive and is made from carbon steel so that it heats quickly, plus it has a natural, "nonstick" type, nano-silica coating (made from sand-blasted crystals). It is a medium gauge, so not too heavy yet not flimsy. It's also scratch resistant, so you can use metal utensils on it, and hydrophobic, which means it repels water, giving your veggies that crisp finish, and oleophilic, which means it allows just enough oil to coat the surface of the wok. It is a clever wok that just gets better with time—I have used mine for over two years now and it is still going strong. It comes with a wooden spatula, a glass lid, and a stainless steel steamer rack. You can purchase it at **www.chinghehuang.com/Lotuswok**

Now you have a wok, what's the first step?
If you don't need to season your new wok, you can go right ahead and start cooking—just use a damp sponge and a little soapy water to wash off any industrial oil, dust, or dirt, then place on the heat to dry. If you need to season your wok, go to my online video at **www.youtube.com/user/chinghehuang**, which shows you how.

The "Breath of the Wok"
I have cooked with a lot of wok masters all over the world and the one thing that differentiates a good stir-fry from a bad one is the "breath of the wok," a term used to describe the *wok-hei*—the "smoky flavor" that comes from a good flame-wokked dish and the all-important balance of *xiang, se, wei* (the aroma, color and taste of the overall dish). This is where home wok cooking differs from restaurant wok cooking. Restaurant wok burners can reach heats of 1200°F and more, far higher than the 350°F that the average domestic burner can achieve, although some powerful domestic burners can go as high as 750°F, but this this by no means exhaustive.

Wok chefs in restaurants maneuver and operate a gas lever by the side of their legs at the same time as they toss the wok and flick it towards the flames so they lick the sides of the wok, injecting wok smoke into the dish. This is why I have so much respect for wok chefs—they have no fear of the flames, which can sometimes be over 6 feet high. They inject the breath of the wok into the dish, as well as sauté, sear, deep-fry, shallow-fry, steam, braise, all in one cooking vessel, and have the eye-to-hand-to-leg body coordination (wok dance) to time the addition of each ingredient perfectly. Cooking over such high heat means that if you are one second off your vegetables lose their shine or crispness and that is why perfect stir-frying is so hard to master. Consistent results take practice, timing, skill, and unwavering focus. However, this doesn't mean that you can't still get those smoky delicious results from wokking at home! I have some tips to help you.

Stir-fry hacks

Freshness is key

Firstly, arm yourself with the freshest ingredients. If ingredients are substandard you will be able to tell, because vegetables will not look fresh and bright and, once stir-fried, they will get limp very quickly.

Preparation is king—no time to stop and chop

When it's wok time, there is no time to do anything—least of all, to stop and chop! So ensure all the ingredients are prepped beforehand and are as close to the wok as possible to save you time.

Size and shape matter

Whenever you add several ingredients to the wok at the same time—for example, aromatics such as garlic, ginger, chiles, and small pieces of onion, or different types of vegetables, such as shredded cabbage, carrots, and onions—it's important they are all a similar size as this will ensure they cook in the same amount of time.

It's important, too, to consider the size of the main protein ingredient in relation to the rest of the ingredients. For example, if you are wokking beef slices, then make sure the vegetables are cut in slices too, so that the dish looks balanced.

All about the cut

How you cut the ingredients is very important. If you slice on a deep diagonal, it exposes more surface area for cooking and it can also make ingredients go that much further. For example, wafer-thin, square-ish slices can be achieved by slicing across the grain of a cut of beef. Vegetables can be prepared in the same way, so a carrot can be sliced into round coins or into long oval pieces if sliced diagonally. Play with the shapes!

"Compartment" cooking

Compartmentalize your ingredients—group aromatics together, also the vegetables and seasonings. Think of your protein and treat it separately—what flavors are you trying to achieve? Finally, think of your garnishes and ways to inject some freshness into the dish at the end.

What level of heat should I go for?

It's important to get your wok really hot before adding anything, so that you see a little smoke rising off the surface. At that point it's time to quickly add the oil, which will heat up instantly. Heating the wok first means the heat is evenly distributed over the entire surface.

Once you add ingredients to it, the temperature in the wok starts to fall a little, but keep the ingredients moving to prevent them from burning or take the wok away from the heat source. If you are really worried about the flame, then heat the wok over medium-high heat and work your way up to maximum heat over the course of several stir-fries where practice becomes perfect.

The right oils

An odorless, flavorless oil that has a high heat point, such as canola oil, peanut oil or coconut oil, is best—it gives a neutral base on which to create your layers of flavor, yet is able to withstand high temperatures. Toasted sesame oil is really only used for seasoning, unless you deliberately wish to "burn" the ingredient, such as the ginger in the Taiwanese recipe "Three cup Chicken" (see page 143).

Balance the aromatics

I like to use a combination of garlic, ginger, and chiles—what I call The Holy Trinity—and sometimes I mix and match them with scallions, shallots, and onions. You can also pair some of these, such as garlic and ginger or ginger and chile. I have been accused of putting garlic, ginger, and chiles in almost all my dishes, but this is because I try to inject their healthful, antibacterial properties into my cooking as much as possible so that I am getting the maximum nutrients in any one meal. But it is entirely up to you and you can vary what you add to suit your likes and mood.

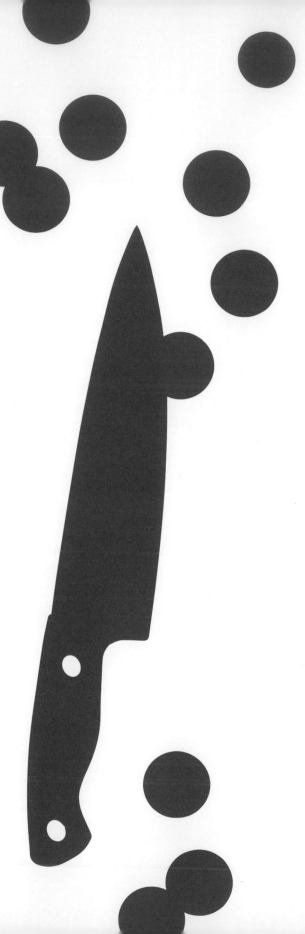

Salt the oil

In my recipes, I sometimes season the oil with a pinch of salt before I add the aromatics. Some chefs swear that this helps to retain the color of the vegetables, and particularly like it as this way are not left with any large flakes of undissolved salt at the end of cooking and the salty flavor is evenly distributed.

Meats

If you are on a budget, you can make meat go further by using the less expensive cuts. The trick is to use a little bit of baking soda—a couple of very small pinches on a tougher piece of rump steak or tough pork thighs, for example, will help to tenderize the meat.

My philosophy on meat is to use free-range or organic where possible; yes, it is expensive but I prefer quality over quantity. Personally, I eat mostly vegetable-based stir-fries during the week so when I do eat meat, I get the good stuff. Eating in this way is a lot healthier (less saturated fat from animal sources), cheaper, and better for the environment too. It is up to you whether you go for the cheaper or expensive meat option, just always make sure you season the meat first, as a pinch of salt, ground white pepper, and a dusting of cornstarch will help the meat taste that much juicier. You can also sometimes add a pinch of spice, whether Chinese five-spice, turmeric, dried chiles, fennel seeds, or ground coriander... just to inject flavor into the meat. You can always taste the difference in the finished dish.

Water is your best friend

When the wok gets too hot to handle, water is your best friend. Having a small bowl or glass of water on hand and knowing when to add a drop is important, especially if the wok gets too hot and you are starting to burn the ingredients. If you are making a one-wok dish where you "don't return" (in Mandarin, *hui guo*) any ingredient to the wok, then you will need to deglaze the wok after cooking individual ingredients and you will need some liquid in between these additions to help each group of ingredients cook. Generally, this is after the protein and again once the vegetables have gone in. When stir frying tender leaf vegetables, after the oil and aromatics have gone in, a small amount of water around the edge of the wok will help to steam-cook the vegetables, ready for seasoning.

Quick homemade sauces and seasonings

From Sriracha and oyster to garlic hoisin, you can create sweet, sour, spicy sauces and dressings that will complement your dishes, whether you use them as cook-in sauces or dressings on the side. I have put together several sauce options (see page 19) so that you can mix and match and also pair them with other dishes to suit your taste buds. Feel free to experiment and chop and change—bring out your inner Tom Cruise in *Cocktail* and think of your condiment cupboard like a bar, where you are the mixologist, creating your own sauces and producing a cocktail of stir-fry flavors. Hippy hippy stir shake, fry!

Soybean pastes

I can't live without my soybean pastes, from fermented salted yellow bean (or whole beans in a jar), chili bean, fermented salted dried black beans (soybeans dried and salted in the sun—just give them a rinse in water, then crush and mix into Shaoxing rice wine to make a paste), to Japanese salty miso paste (which comes in red and white varieties—great for soups, stir-fries, sauces, dressings, and marinades), and the Korean chili paste *gochujang*, which, together with the Korean yellow bean paste, *doenjang*, is one of my favorites. The flavor combinations are limitless, with endless umami (deep savory) possibilities…

Curry and spice pastes

I love to experiment with Southeast Asian curry pastes such as Thai red curry, Thai green curry, yellow curry, and so on, and not just to make curry, but for stir-frying and in noodle soups. I also love chili pastes and sambals from Malaysia, as well as spice mixes and tamarind paste, which give a sour kick and an exotic Southeast Asian taste to my dishes.

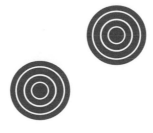

Make it shine

Cornstarch or potato flour is an all-important store cupboard ingredient because it helps to bind the flavors in the wok to the protein and vegetables. Traditionally, when cooking meats, a technique called "velveting" was the norm. It involved coating chicken or beef strips with egg white and cornstarch to give the meat a silky texture so it retained its juiciness when shallow fried. However, I've developed a new way to enhance the flavor of the meat without the shallow-frying step—I season the meat first with salt and ground white pepper, then dust with cornstarch or potato flour. This helps to seal in the juices of the meat as it hits the oil in the wok. To ensure the ingredient doesn't stick in the wok, let it sear for 10 seconds, then, once it has some color, you can easily flip the meat to cook on the other side. Don't worry if the meat catches—those slightly burnt edges all add to the flavor. You can also loosen the flavors in the wok by using a small drop of water or Shaoxing rice wine to deglaze the pan after cooking the meat.

In some of the dishes, the cornstarch is also mixed with cold water to create a blended cornstarch paste that is usually added at the end of the cooking to thicken the sauce and give it a shine as it comes to a boil.

In many dishes, where I "compartmentalize" and group ingredients together for a more complex flavor, I like to add the cornstarch to the ingredients for the sauce—just ensure that the main liquid in the sauce, whether it's water or vegetable stock, is cold, so that the sauce has not thickened before it's been added to the wok (you want the sauce to thicken and caramelize in the wok, not before in the bowl).

Love your dofu (or is it tofu)?

The Mandarin transliteration is "dofu," the Japanese is tofu. However, whether you call it dofu or tofu, there is no doubt that it is a good source of protein and contains all nine essential amino acids. It is also an excellent source of iron, calcium, manganese, selenium, and phosphorus, and of copper, magnesium, vitamin B1, and zinc. Whether you choose fresh, fried, smoked, firm, or soft, tofu offers a great meat substitute for vegan and vegetarian meals and is an important food source for Buddhists—it features heavily in Buddhist Chinese cuisine. Try to get organic tofu or tofu made from sprouted soy.

Spices

To get the best out your spices, particularly whole spices such as Sichuan peppercorns, first dry-toast them in a wok or small pan and then grind them in a mortar and pestle or coffee grinder.

Adding an aromatic flourish

Whether you do so with scallions, fresh cilantro, mint, raw bean sprouts, nuts or seeds, Japanese nori seaweed, chile flakes, or a wedge of lemon or lime, adding a fragrant aromatic garnish to your stir-fry at the end will enhance your dish.

> TIP: The nutritional analysis of cal, carbs, protein and fat is per portion.

Rice and nutritious grains

Most of the dishes in this book will pair well with rice, unless it's a chow mein. You can also use other grains and legumes mixed into the rice too, which is something I like to do when I am trying to eat more healthily. For example, I often mix jasmine rice, wild rice, and green lentils. At other times I serve plain jasmine rice for comfort, and basmati is a good option for fried rice, as it is more robust. Brown rice is also delicious and high in fiber and can be mixed with jasmine rice, wild rice, and chickpeas to create a different bite.

Noodles

It's best to precook noodles according to the package instructions, then drain them and drizzle with some toasted sesame oil to prevent them from sticking together. For low-carb and wheat-free options, try mung bean noodles, sweet potato noodles, shirataki, and rice noodles. I also love the traditional wheat flour noodles, which come in several varieties, such as buckwheat, somen, ramen, udon, and egg. Recently, I've discovered high protein organic gluten-free soybean noodles, which are delicious in noodle soups, salads, and, of course, stir-fries.

> **TIPS:** Use organic or free-range chicken and eggs as they will taste better. All eggs used in these recipes are medium.
>
> Many dishes are gluten-free if you use tamari instead of light soy sauce.

Order of ingredients

When stir-frying, you want the aromatics to impart their essence into the dish without burning them, the meat to be tender and cooked through, and the vegetables to remain crisp and fresh. The order, therefore, in which each ingredient is added and the timing of each addition is vital. There are so many different stir-fries that it is impossible to give a set blueprint—it really does depend on what you are creating. However, there are a few simple rules and methods that are useful to bear in mind as you wok away and start to improvise:

Vegetable stir-fry
(*Cao Cai*)

1

Heat the wok, add the oil, then the aromatics, and stir-fry for a few seconds to impart their aroma.

2

Add the vegetables—the crunchier ones first—and stir-fry for less than a minute. Then add the more tender vegetables, cooking them for less than 30 seconds or until wilted. Add a little water around the edges of the wok to create some steam and aid the cooking process.

3

Then it's quickly on to a seasoning liquid of your choice. Cook for 5 seconds, then give a final toss to ensure a balanced, seasoned dish.

Dry meat stir-fry
(*Gan Rou Cao*)

1

Heat the wok, add the oil, then the aromatics, and stir-fry for a few seconds.

2

Add meat slices (seasoned with spices and dredged in cornstarch or marinated and dredged in potato flour). Allow the meat to "settle" (sear on one side) in the wok, before flipping it over to cook on the other side for a few seconds.

3

Deglaze the wok with some Shaoxing rice wine or dry sherry, stock, or water, then toss in seasoning ingredients, such as soy sauce, chili sauce, or sesame oil, and cook for 30 seconds. A final toss ensures a balanced, seasoned dish. Garnish with fresh herbs (cilantro, scallions, or chives) and serve immediately.

Saucy Meat & Veggie Stir-fry
(Gou Chien Rou Cai)

1

Heat the wok, add the oil, then the aromatics, and stir-fry for a few seconds.

2

Add the meat slices (seasoned with salt and ground white pepper and dredged in potato flour). Allow the meat to "settle" (sear on one side) in the wok, before flipping it over to cook on the other side for a few seconds.

3

Deglaze the wok with some Shaoxing rice wine or dry sherry, stock, or water, then toss in your vegetables (all cut into similar shapes and sizes).

4

Pour in a cup of vegetable stock, add seasoning ingredients, such as light soy sauce, black rice vinegar, toasted sesame oil, and chili sauces. Bring the liquid to a boil, season with cornstarch and water paste, and give a final toss to ensure a balanced, seasoned dish. Garnish with fresh herbs (if using) and serve immediately.

Stir-fry noodles
(Cao mein)

1

Heat the wok, add the oil, then the aromatics, and stir-fry for a few seconds.

2

Add the meat slices (seasoned with salt and ground white pepper and dredged in potato flour). Allow the meat to "settle" (sear on one side) in the wok, before flipping it over to cook on the other side for a few seconds.

3

Deglaze the wok with some Shaoxing rice wine or dry sherry, stock, or water, then toss in your vegetables (all cut into similar shapes and sizes).

4

Add the cooked noodles, followed by seasoning ingredients, such as light soy sauce, black rice vinegar, toasted sesame oil, or chili sauce. Stir-fry for 1 minute, mixing all the ingredients well, then give a final toss to ensure a balanced, seasoned dish. Garnish with fresh herbs (if using), and serve immediately.

Stir-fry "Soup" Noodles
(Tang Mein)

1

Heat the wok, add the oil, then the aromatics, and stir-fry for a few seconds.

2

Add the meat slices (seasoned with salt and ground white pepper and dredged in potato flour). Allow the meat to "settle" (sear on one side) in the wok, before flipping it over to cook on the other side for a few seconds.

3

Deglaze the wok with some Shaoxing rice wine or dry sherry, stock, or water, then toss in your vegetables (all cut into similar shapes and sizes).

4

Pour in 3½ cups vegetable stock, add cooked noodles, seasoning ingredients, such as light soy sauce, black rice vinegar, toasted sesame oil, or chili sauce. Bring to a boil, season with cornstarch and water paste. Give a final toss, garnish with fresh herbs (if using), and serve immediately.

Fried Rice
(*Cao Fan*)

1

Heat the wok, add the oil, and scramble some lightly seasoned eggs. Remove from the wok and set aside.

2

Reheat the wok, add more oil, then the aromatics, and stir-fry for a few seconds.

3

Add small pieces of meat (seasoned with salt, ground white pepper or dredged in potato flour). Allow the meat to "settle" (sear on one side) in the wok, before flipping it over to cook on the other side for a few seconds.

4

Deglaze the wok with some Shaoxing rice wine or dry sherry, stock or water, then toss in finely diced vegetables, and cooked rice, followed by seasoning ingredients, such as light soy sauce, black rice vinegar, toasted sesame oil or chili sauce. Cook for 1 minute, add the scrambled eggs, and then give a final toss to ensure a balanced seasoned dish, garnish with fresh herbs (if using) and serve immediately.

Saucy tricks

Sesame Oil, Vinegar, Soy Sauce

a.k.a dumpling sauce

1 part toasted sesame oil
1 part rice or cider vinegar
1 part soy sauce

Mix together in a small glass jar or bowl.

Soy Lemon Chili Oil

Delicious as a dressing.

1 part soy sauce
1 part chili oil
1 part lemon juice

Mix together in a small glass jar or bowl.

Oyster Sauce Ketchup

Great on a burger.

1 part oyster sauce
1 part ketchup

Mix together in a small glass jar or bowl.

Salty Spicy Sriracha

Use as seasoning in a stir-fry or as a sauce to pour over steamed vegetables.

1 part soy sauce
1 part Sriracha chili sauce

Mix together in a small glass jar or bowl.

Black Rice Vinegar, Chili, and Soy

Use as seasoning for fried rice or chow mein.

1 part Chinkiang black rice vinegar or balsamic vinegar
1 part chili sauce
1 part soy sauce

Mix together in a small glass jar or bowl.

Sesame Soy

Use as seasoning for stir-fried vegetables.

1 part toasted sesame oil
1 part soy sauce

Mix together in a small glass jar or bowl.

Soy Sesame Ginger Miso

Use as a dressing on steamed fish.

1 part soy sauce
1 part toasted sesame oil
¼ part freshly grated ginger
1 part miso

Mix together in a small glass jar or bowl.

My top wok tips

Stir-fry to health

The healthiest way to sear food at high heat, stir-frying retains the nutrients in food for maximum flavor, with minimum effort required.

Steamed not stirred

Steam chicken, fish, or tofu together with your favorite vegetables, marinated in a healthy Chinese sauce, for a healthy one-wok supper. If it's easy to cook, you'll be likely to do it again. Consistently eat this way and you'll be beaming with health.

Rice and grains baby

Try to mix several different kinds of rice for texture, flavor, and nutrients. I often combine jasmine, brown rice, wild rice, and red rice, and sometimes include lentils and chickpeas for maximum protein.

Know your oils

Use only a small amount of a good heat-stable oil such as coconut, canola, or peanut oil, all of which are perfect for stir-frying over high heat. Save your virgin olive oils for delicious dressings.

Magic mushrooms

The Chinese are obsessed with dried shiitake mushrooms; not only do they have an earthy, savory umami flavor, they are also full of minerals and nutrients. So throw them into broths and soups for healthy tonics.

Berry excited

The Chinese goji berry contains essential amino acids, as well as the highest concentration of protein of any fruit. Loaded with vitamin C and carotenoids, it has 21 trace minerals and is also high in fiber. Throw some into a stir-fry or over steamed fish for a sweet pop.

Go nuts

I love to add cashews, pine nuts, walnuts, and Brazils to my stir-fries. Nuts contain healthy fats, are high in protein, and a good source of minerals and vitamin E, which promotes healthy skin. A small handful in any dish is enough. You can toast or roast your own to give an extra layer of flavor; just step away from the salted variety.

Get fruity and saucy

I like to mix naturally brewed soy sauce with different kinds of fruit juices and fresh or dried chiles for a sweet-savory spicy taste to my dishes. A great combination is soy sauce, pineapple juice, chile flakes, and honey. You can also use fresh orange juice, grape juice, mango juice, and apple juice.

Spice it up

Chinese five-spice, which is made up of cloves, cinnamon, star anise, Sichuan peppercorns, and fennel, adds a distinctive pungent, sweet, spicy, bitter, and sour note to dishes. Use it to marinate meats—add with soy sauce and olive oil and some cornstarch to coat. The spices come with zero calories and are sealed when they hit the wok, giving hot hits of flavor.

Wok on!

Invest in a good wok. My nano-silica coated Lotus wok (see page 9) does not give off PFOA and PTFE (perfluorooctanoic acid and polytetrafluoroethylene fumes), toxic chemical fumes that are hazardous to the human body, and you only need a small amount of oil to cook up a great tasting meal. It's also hydrophobic, which means it repels water, and oleophilic, which means it absorbs the right amount of oil to keep your veggies crisp and delicious.

Flavorful toppings

In Mandarin, cooked ingredients that add a bold hit of flavor to dishes are called *zu xiang*. In Taiwanese they are known as *ken pung*. Usually cooked in oil to explode their flavors, they are either incorporated into finished dishes or served as a condiment on the side.

Soy Shiitake Mushrooms

Use dried shiitake mushrooms, which carry the most flavor.

1 tablespoon canola oil
knob of fresh ginger, peeled and grated
5 small shallots, finely chopped
3½ ounces dried shiitake mushrooms, soaked in warm water for 20 minutes, then drained, tough stalks discarded, and finely diced
2 tablespoons low-sodium light soy sauce
1 teaspoon toasted sesame oil
pinch of superfine sugar

Heat a wok over high heat until smoking and add the canola oil. Add the ginger and shallots and stir-fry for a few seconds, then add the diced shiitake mushrooms and toss for 1 minute until the shallots have softened. Add the light soy sauce and cook over medium heat until the shallots and mushrooms have absorbed the flavor of the soy and caramelized at the edges. Season with the toasted sesame oil and a pinch of superfine sugar. Place in a small bowl and serve with rice and vegetables, or serve some on top of your favorite chow mein.

Fried Chile Dried Shrimp

3 tablespoons canola oil
1 red chile, seeded and finely chopped
1 scallion, finely sliced into ½-inch rounds
3½ ounces dried baby shrimp, soaked in hot water for 20 minutes, then drained, dried, and very finely diced
pinch of sea salt flakes
pinch of dried chile flakes

Heat a wok over high heat until smoking and add the canola oil. Add the chile and scallion and toss for a few seconds to release their flavors. Add the dried baby shrimp and stir-fry for 2 minutes until the shrimp is a little golden at the edges and toasted. Season with the salt and dried chile flakes. Spoon out and serve on top of rice, stir-fried vegetables, or noodles.

Fried Garlic and Shallots

⅓ cup potato flour
pinch of sea salt flakes
pinch of ground white pepper
pinch of vegetable bouillon powder
5 garlic cloves, sliced
5 small shallots, sliced
½ cup canola oil

Put the potato flour, some sea salt, white pepper, and the bouillon powder into a bowl and mix well. Toss the garlic cloves and shallots in the seasoned flour and sieve out into another bowl.

Add the oil to the wok and heat to 350°F or until a piece of bread dropped in turns golden brown in 15 seconds. Using a small spider or slotted spoon, gently lower the garlic and shallots into the oil. Fry for 20 seconds until golden, then lift out with the spoon and drain on paper towels. Season further to taste with salt, pepper, and vegetable bouillon powder. Sprinkle on top of meat, shellfish, noodles, or fried rice dishes.

Chinese Salted Black Bean Cooked "Salsa"

This Chinese salsa is not cooked all the way through so you can appreciate the salty bite and flavors of each of the ingredients.

3 tablespoons canola oil
pinch of sea salt flakes
2 garlic cloves, finely chopped
knob of fresh ginger, peeled and grated
1 red chile, seeded and finely chopped
2 scallions, finely chopped
1 tablespoon fermented salted black beans, rinsed and crushed
2 tablespoons Shaoxing rice wine or dry sherry
1 teaspoon low-sodium light soy sauce

Heat a wok over high heat until smoking and add the canola oil. Add the salt and let it dissolve in the hot oil. Add the garlic, ginger, chile, and scallions and toss for a few seconds, then add the fermented salted black beans and toss for 1 minute to release their flavors. Add the Shaoxing rice wine or dry sherry and season with the light soy sauce. This is delicious over fish, chicken, and wok-fried beef, or added to noodles, vegetables, and rice dishes.

Braised Red-cooked Sweet and Sour Shallots

10 mini shallots, left whole
1¾ cups cold water
½ cup cold vegetable stock
¼ cup low-sodium light soy sauce
1 tablespoon Chinkiang black rice vinegar or balsamic vinegar
1 teaspoon dark soy sauce
2 tablespoons brown sugar
1 cinnamon stick
1 star anise

Heat a wok over medium heat, add all the ingredients, and cook for 20 minutes until the liquid has reduced by half and the shallots are soft and tender but still hold their shape. Remove the cinnamon stick and star anise. Serve with rice, vegetables, or noodles.

Pickles and chili sauces

You can add these on the side to pimp up your stir-fries. And why not try some pickles and chili sauces—easy to make and full of flavor.

Sichuan Garlic Cucumber "Pickle"

4 small cucumbers, halved lengthwise and cut into half-moon slices
1 tablespoon toasted white sesame seeds

For the marinade
2 garlic cloves, grated
¼ cup rice or cider vinegar
¼ cup mirin
pinch of ground dry-toasted Sichuan peppercorns
pinch of dried chile flakes
1 teaspoon chili oil
pinch of sea salt flakes

Mix all the ingredients for the marinade in a small bowl. Place the cucumbers on a shallow pan/bowl, pour the marinade over them, and pickle for 10 minutes. Serve on top of fried noodles, rice, meat, or shellfish.

Fried Chile Okra

2 tablespoons canola oil
3 green chiles, seeded and finely chopped
1 cup okra, sliced into ⅛-inch coins
1 tablespoon Shaoxing rice wine or dry sherry
2 tablespoons low-sodium light soy sauce
1 tablespoon Chinkiang black rice vinegar or balsamic vinegar
pinch of superfine sugar

Heat a wok over high heat until smoking and add the canola oil. Add the chiles and toss for a few seconds to release their flavor. Add the okra and cook for less than 1 minute. Season with the rice wine, soy sauce, vinegar, and superfine sugar and cook for 30 seconds until the okra is tender, yet still has a slight bite and the liquid in the wok has reduced. Serve on rice or noodles, or toss some into your favorite steamed greens.

Sweet and Sour Tomato "Sambal"

2 garlic cloves, crushed
knob of fresh ginger, peeled and coarsely chopped
2 red chiles, seeds in, coarsely chopped
1 tablespoon tomato paste
1 tablespoon low-sodium light soy sauce
2 tablespoons agave syrup
½ teaspoon dried chile flakes
¼ cup cold water
2 tablespoons canola oil
pinch of sea salt flakes
lime juice

Put the garlic, ginger, chiles, tomato paste, soy sauce, agave syrup, chile flakes, and water into a food processor and pulse to a paste.

Heat a wok over medium heat and add the oil, then the paste, and simmer for 2 to 3 minutes. Season to taste with salt and lime juice.

Serve on the side of your favorite stir-fry.

Sweet and Sour Plum Daikon

2 ripe plums, pitted and finely
    chopped
1 tablespoon superfine sugar
1 star anise
juice of ½ lime
7 ounces daikon, peeled and
    grated (about 1¼ cups)

Pour ¾ cup water into a pan
and add the plums, sugar, and
star anise. Bring to a boil, then
turn the heat down to a simmer
and cook for 10 minutes.
Remove from the heat. Strain
the ingredients over a bowl and
collect the plum sauce, then
stir in the lime juice.

Put the daikon in a shallow
bowl, pour the sweet and sour
plum sauce over it, and leave
for 10 minutes to pickle. Serve
with fried spicy dishes for a
fresh sweet and sour bite.

Vegetables

V DF

Wok-fried Cauliflower with Honey Soy Hoisin and Pine Nuts

For the sauce
1 teaspoon freshly grated peeled ginger
1 red chile, seeded and finely chopped
1 teaspoon honey
1 tablespoon hoisin sauce
1 teaspoon low-sodium light soy sauce
¼ cup cold vegetable stock
1 tablespoon cornstarch combined with 2 tablespoons cold water

For the stir-fry
1 tablespoon canola oil
1 head of cauliflower, washed and broken into florets

For the garnish
handful of toasted pine nuts
handful of finely chopped chives

The trick here is to wok-char the cauliflower to bring out its smoky, sweet flavors. Then, with the spicy, savory hoisin sauce, the pungent chives and the crunchy pine nuts, it's a deeply satisfying dish—perfect with noodles or rice, or even on its own.

Serves 2 cal 310 carbs 30g protein 10.1g fat 17.3g

Whisk together all the ingredients for the sauce in a small bowl, then set aside.

Heat a wok over high heat until smoking and add the canola oil. Add the cauliflower florets and stir-fry for 30 seconds, then drizzle in 2 tablespoons cold water around the edge of the wok to create some steam to help cook the florets. Keep stirring until any liquid evaporates, charring the florets.

Pour in the sauce and stir carefully to coat the florets well. Bring the sauce to a boil and cook until glossy and the cauliflower is tender, for about 4 minutes.

Finally, garnish with the pine nuts and chopped chives and serve.

Spicy Soy Mushroom Tofu

1 tablespoon canola oil

2 garlic cloves, finely chopped

knob of fresh ginger, peeled and finely grated

14 ounces fresh firm tofu, drained and sliced into ¾-inch cubes

1 tablespoon Shaoxing rice wine or dry sherry

2 tablespoons tamari

1 tablespoon mushroom "oyster" sauce

1 teaspoon Sriracha chili sauce

1 tablespoon rice vinegar or cider vinegar

For the garnish and to serve

3 tablespoons chopped chives

1 teaspoon shimichi pepper flakes or dried chile flakes

Tofu can be boring but here it is enhanced by many layers of Chinese flavors—bittersweet Shaoxing rice wine, umami tamari, rich, earthy mushroom sauce and tangy sriracha heat— which all combine to make this a true vegan winner. It's perfect on a veggie bibimbap (a Korean rice dish) or with plain rice and pickles on the side.

Serves 2 cal 258 carbs 9.3g protein 21.4g fat 14.3g

Heat a wok over high heat until smoking and add the canola oil. Add the garlic and ginger and fry for a few seconds, then add the tofu cubes. Stir-fry for 1 minute to brown, then add the Shaoxing rice wine or dry sherry.

Season with the tamari, mushroom "oyster" sauce, Sriracha, and vinegar and gently toss, then flip the tofu over, being careful not to break up the pieces, and cook for 1 minute.

Garnish with the chopped chives and shimichi pepper and serve.

20 mins*

5 mins

*includes cooking the rice

V Ve DF

Shiitake, Kimchi, and Pineapple Fried Rice

1 tablespoon canola oil

knob of fresh ginger, peeled and grated

5 large fresh shiitake mushrooms, rinsed, patted dry, and cut into thin slices, stalks optional

½ teaspoon dark soy sauce

1 tablespoon fermented cucumber kimchi, finely sliced

1½ cups cooked brown rice (¾ cup uncooked)

2 tablespoons low-sodium light soy sauce

¾ cup fresh pineapple, finely diced into cubes

1 to 2 tablespoons sliced scallions, to garnish

A delicious sweet, umami-flavored fried rice. Perfect for dinner, any night of the week.

Serves 2 cal 291 carbs 51.8g protein 7.4g fat 7.3g

Heat a wok over high heat until smoking and add the canola oil. Add the grated ginger and stir-fry for 5 seconds, then add the shiitake mushrooms and stir-fry for 30 seconds.

Season with the dark soy sauce, then add the sliced cucumber kimchi followed by the cooked rice and toss together for 1 minute.

Season with the light soy sauce, then add the fresh pineapple cubes and toss gently into the rice. Garnish with the scallions and serve immediately.

Wok-fried Radicchio with Jicama, Blood Orange, Pomelo, and Cashews

1 tablespoon canola oil

1 garlic clove, finely chopped

10 ounces radicchio, washed and torn into bite-sized pieces

1 teaspoon fried-garlic shallots (see page 22)

1 teaspoon low-sodium light soy sauce

For the garnish

¼ cup peeled and grated jicama

1 ripe blood orange, peeled and segmented

segments from ¼ pomelo or grapefruit

1 small handful roasted, salted cashews

zest and juice of 1 lime

A fresh and zingy wok-cooked dish, perfect for hot summer days. Sear the radicchio in the wok for a charred smoky flavor and, if you can't get jicama, use grated crunchy apples or pears instead.

Serves 2 cal 197 carbs 18.7g protein 4.6g fat 13.2g

Heat a wok over high heat until smoking and add the canola oil and garlic, and stir-fry for 5 seconds. Add the radicchio and toss for 5 seconds until slightly charred and wilted. Toss in the garlic-fried shallots and add the light soy sauce.

Garnish with the grated jicama, blood orange segments, pomelo or grapefruit segments, and cashews. Sprinkle with the lime zest and squeeze over the lime juice. Serve immediately.

*includes cooking the noodles

V DF

Vegetarian Hokkien Mee

1 tablespoon canola oil
2 garlic cloves, finely chopped
knob of fresh ginger, peeled
    and grated
2 mini sweet shallots, finely
    chopped
1 red chile, seeded and finely
    chopped
3 dried Chinese mushrooms,
    soaked in warm water for
    20 minutes, drained, stalks
    discarded, and finely diced
¾ cup Quorn grounds or other
    soy protein crumbles
1 teaspoon dark soy sauce
½ cup hot vegetable stock
1 tablespoon low-sodium light
    soy sauce
drizzle of toasted sesame oil
2 cups cooked Chinese egg
    noodles (7 ounces dried)

For the garnish
1 cup fresh bean sprouts,
    blanched in boiling water for
    10 seconds, rinsed in cold
    water, and drained
red chile, sliced into rings
    (optional)
scallions, trimmed and sliced
    ¾-inch on a diagonal

Hokkien Mee is a Malaysian Chinese dish that is usually topped with pork and shrimp and served on Chinese egg noodles. My vegetarian version swaps the meat and shellfish for braised Chinese mushrooms and ground soy protein and, in my opinion, they provide a rich, savory topping that is just as good. It's delicious garnished with scallions, which add a fresh bite, and a little red chile for an extra kick.

Serves 2 cal 493 carbs 66.5g protein 20.2g fat 16.2g

Heat a wok over high heat until smoking and add the canola oil. Add the garlic, ginger, shallots, and chile and explode the flavors in the wok for a few seconds. Add the diced Chinese mushrooms and the Quorn grounds or protein crumbles and season with the dark soy sauce to enrich the color. Add the vegetable stock and light soy sauce and let cook for 10 minutes until the sauce has reduced.

Meanwhile, drizzle some toasted sesame oil over the cooked egg noodles. Divide the noodles between two bowls, then top with the mushroom and Quorn mixture, and garnish with bean sprouts, fresh chiles, and sliced scallions. Serve immediately.

* includes soaking
the mushrooms

V Ve DF

1 tablespoon canola oil
knob of fresh ginger, peeled
    and grated
1 red chile, seeded and finely
    chopped
¾-ounce wood ear mushrooms,
    soaked in hot water for
    20 minutes, then drained
    and sliced into thin strips
10 ounces Chinese cabbage,
    such as Napa, stalks removed
    and cut into 1-inch slices
1 tablespoon Shaoxing rice wine
    or dry sherry
½ cup vegetable stock
1 tablespoon low-sodium light
    soy sauce
½ teaspoon dark soy sauce
1 tablespoon rice vinegar or
    cider vinegar
1 tablespoon cornstarch blended
    with 2 tablespoons cold water
2 scallions, sliced into julienne
    strips

Hot and Sour Chinese Cabbage

This is a beautifully warming winter dish, perfect served with rice or poured on top of thin wheat noodles. The spicy hot and sour notes of the dish make it incredibly flavorful and addictive.

Serves 2 cal 150 carbs 20.6g protein 3.2g fat 6.4g

Heat a wok over high heat until smoking and add the canola oil. Add the ginger and chile and stir-fry for a few seconds, then add the wood ear mushrooms and Chinese cabbage and toss for 1 minute. Drizzle 2 tablespoons cold water around the edge of the wok to create some steam to help cook the vegetables.

Add the Shaoxing rice wine or dry sherry, then pour in the vegetable stock and season with the light and dark soy sauces and the vinegar. Bring to a boil, then add the blended cornstarch and stir to thicken.

Garnish with the sliced scallions and serve immediately.

V Ve DF

Sichuan Smoked Tofu Gan with Celery and Roasted Peanuts

1 tablespoon canola oil
1 garlic clove, minced
1 teaspoon ground dry-toasted Sichuan peppercorns
Chinese celery ribs and leaves, or celery, cut diagonally into slices ¼-inch thick
7-ounce piece of firm tofu gan (dried firm smoked bean curd), cut into ⅛-inch thick slices
1 teaspoon chili bean paste
1 tablespoon Chinkiang black rice vinegar or balsamic vinegar
1 tablespoon low-sodium light soy sauce
1 tablespoon chili oil
pinch of freshly ground white pepper
juice of ½ lemon

For the garnish
small handful of roasted peanuts, crushed
small handful of fresh cilantro, finely chopped

This dish delivers a deliciously spicy vegan hit that is perfect served with boiled rice and a scattering of crunchy peanuts.

Serves 2 cal 351 carbs 7.6g protein 20.8g fat 26.4g

Heat a wok over high heat until smoking and add the canola oil. Add the garlic and ground Sichuan peppercorns and stir-fry for 5 seconds. Add the celery and stir-fry for 1 minute until softened, then add the tofu slices and carefully toss until heated through—about 1 minute.

Add the rest of the seasoning sauce: chili bean paste, Chinkiang rice vinegar, light soy sauce, and the chili oil and toss well. Season with the light soy sauce, plus the chili oil, ground white pepper, and a squeeze of lemon juice and toss again.

Transfer to a serving plate and sprinkle with the crushed peanuts and chopped cilantro. Serve immediately.

V Ve DF

Tofu, Tomato, Mushroom, and Scallion Scramble

1 tablespoon canola oil

2 large ripe tomatoes, each cored and cut into 6 wedges

3½ ounces shimeji mushrooms

1 tablespoon Shaoxing rice wine or dry sherry

9 ounces fresh firm tofu, drained and very lightly broken up using a fork

pinch of ground turmeric

pinch of dried chile flakes

1 tablespoon low-sodium light soy sauce

pinch of sea salt flakes

pinch of ground black pepper

1 scallion, sliced on the diagonal, to garnish

This is a real homestyle dish and reminds me of my grandmother's cooking. It's a bit like making scrambled eggs but using tofu as the star. This scramble is vegan friendly and should be light and fluffy; it's delicious served with steamed rice.

Serves 2 cal 191 carbs 8.4g protein 13.7g fat 11.2g

Heat a wok over high heat until smoking and add the canola oil. Add the tomatoes and stir-fry for 1 minute until softened, then add the shimeji mushrooms and stir-fry for another minute until browned.

Season with the Shaoxing rice wine or dry sherry, then add the tofu and stir in to mix well. Season with the turmeric and dried chile flakes and cook for 1 minute. Add the light soy sauce and toss, cooking until it has covered the tofu, then season with salt and black pepper.

Garnish with the scallions and serve immediately on its own or with steamed rice.

* includes chilling time

V Ve DF

Sichuan Haricots Verts on Chilled Silken Tofu

1 tablespoon canola oil

knob of fresh ginger, peeled and grated

1 teaspoon ground, dry-toasted Sichuan peppercorns

1 medium red chile, seeded and finely chopped

7 ounces haricots verts, sliced into ¼-inch rounds (about 2 cups)

1 tablespoon lemon juice

1 tablespoon rice vinegar or cider vinegar

1 tablespoon low-sodium light soy sauce

1 tablespoon chili oil

1 teaspoon toasted sesame oil

14 ounces ready-to-eat, firm silken tofu, drained and sliced into ½-inch cubes, chilled for 20 minutes, and served as one block

small handful of fresh cilantro stems and leaves, finely chopped, to garnish

This is a great way to cook green beans but it is important they are fresh. When you buy them, snap one in half and, if it makes a crunchy snap, you know they are at their best. This dish is very quick to prepare and the contrast between the hot, spicy beans and the chilled, silken tofu is delicious. Serve with steamed rice or enjoy simply on its own.

Serves 2 cal 276 carbs 9.1g protein 17.1g fat 18.5g

Heat a wok over high heat until smoking and add the canola oil. Add the ginger, Sichuan pepper, and red chile and toss for a few seconds.

Add the green beans and toss well, then add a small splash of cold water to create some steam to help cook the beans. Toss for 2 to 3 minutes until the beans are tender, then season with the lemon juice, vinegar, light soy sauce, and the chili and toasted sesame oils, and take off the heat.

Place the chilled silken tofu in a bowl and slice into small cubes. Pour the beans over the top, garnish with the chopped cilantro leaves and stems, and serve immediately.

V Ve DF

Edamame Mapo Tofu

For the sauce
¾ cup cold vegetable stock
1 tablespoon Chinkiang black
    rice vinegar or balsamic
    vinegar
1 teaspoon low sodium light
    soy sauce
1 tablespoon cornstarch

For the stir-fry
1 tablespoon canola oil
2 garlic cloves, crushed and
    finely chopped
1 tablespoon fresh ginger, peeled
    and grated
1 medium red chile, seeded and
    finely chopped
1¼ cups edamame beans
14 ounces fresh firm tofu,
    drained and cut into 1-inch
    chunks
2 tablespoons chili bean sauce
1 tablespoon Shaoxing rice wine
    or dry sherry
pinch of sea salt flakes
pinch of ground white pepper
pinch of ground dry-toasted
    Sichuan peppercorns
2 large scallions, cut into julienne
    slices and soaked in iced
    water to curl

Mapo tofu is a Sichuanese dish named after a famous Sichuan vendor who was recognized by her pockmarked appearance— this dish is traditionally also known as "Mrs. Pockmarked Tofu". The classic version uses ground pork and sometimes ground beef. However, I like to use some edamame beans instead, which add a satisfying bite in contrast to the soft tofu. This is a delicious recipe through and through, and is great served with plain boiled rice to soak up the spicy sauce.

Serves 2 cal 467 carbs 27.4g protein 33.2g fat 23.4g

Whisk together all the ingredients for the sauce in a bowl, then set aside.

Heat a wok over high heat and as the wok starts to smoke, add the canola oil. Add the garlic, ginger, and chopped chile and stir-fry to explode the flavors. Add the edamame and stir-fry for a few seconds, then add the tofu and toss, cooking for a few more seconds.

Add the chili bean paste and the Shaoxing rice wine and cook for 1 minute, then add the sauce. Bring to a boil and cook until thickened. Season further to taste with the salt, ground white pepper, and ground Sichuan peppercorns, then stir and add the scallions. Serve immediately.

5 mins

8–9 mins

V Ve DF

Kung Po Tofu

For the sauce

½ cup cold vegetable stock

1 tablespoon low-sodium light soy sauce

1 tablespoon ketchup

1 tablespoon Chinkiang black rice vinegar or balsamic vinegar

1 teaspoon Sriracha chili sauce or good chili sauce

1 tablespoon cornstarch

For the stir-fry

1 tablespoon canola oil

1 tablespoon Sichuan peppercorns

3 whole dried chiles

7 ounces fried tofu, cut into ¾-inch cubes

1 tablespoon Shaoxing rice wine or dry sherry

1 small red bell pepper, seeded and chopped into small chunks

handful of dry roasted peanuts or cashews

2 scallions, sliced on an angle

This is a great Sichuan dish that was invented by Ding Baozhen, the dearly loved governor of Sichuan in the nineteenth century. Its numbing, spicy sweet and tangy flavors are delicious with crispy fried tofu or, if you like meat, fry seasoned chicken strips first, then follow the rest of the steps. Also, if you'd prefer a healthier alternative to fried tofu, use smoked firm tofu instead.

Serves 2 cal 470 carbs 23g protein 28.9g fat 30.3g

Whisk together all the ingredients for the sauce in a small glass bowl, then set aside.

Heat a wok over high heat until smoking and add the canola oil. Add the Sichuan peppercorns and dried chiles and stir-fry for a few seconds, then add the fried tofu cubes and stir-fry for 1 minute until the tofu is seared at the edges. Add the Shaoxing rice wine or dry sherry, then add the red bell pepper and cook for less than 30 seconds.

Give the sauce a quick stir, then pour into the wok and bring to a boil. When the sauce has reduced, is slightly sticky, and has a thicker consistency, add the peanuts or cashews followed by the scallions and cook for 1 minute. Stir together well, then transfer to a serving plate and serve immediately.

*** includes soaking
the mushrooms**

Ⓥ Ⓥ̲ₑ ⅅⅎ

Black Bean Buddha's Stir-fried Mixed Vegetables

For the sauce

½ cup cold vegetable stock

1 tablespoon low-sodium light
    soy sauce

1 tablespoon vegetarian
    mushroom sauce

1 teaspoon toasted sesame oil

1 tablespoon cornstarch

For the stir-fry

1 tablespoon canola oil

knob of fresh ginger, peeled and
    grated

½ teaspoon fermented salted
    black beans, rinsed, then
    crushed with 1 tablespoon
    Shaoxing rice wine or dry
    sherry

1 medium carrot, cut into
    julienne strips

4 fresh shiitake mushrooms,
    rinsed, dried, and sliced

small handful of dried wood ear
    mushrooms, soaked in hot
    water for 20 minutes, drained,
    and sliced into ½-inch strips

small handful of baby corn, sliced
    in half on a diagonal

1 x 8-ounce can of bamboo
    shoots, drained and cut into
    julienne strips

small handful of fresh bean
    sprouts

2 scallions, finely sliced, to
    garnish

Buddha's Stir-fried Mixed Vegetables is a famous Chinese dish that is served at all important Chinese festivals throughout the year. Typically a dish such as this would contain straw mushrooms and dried lily flowers. You can use a bag of mixed stir-fry vegetables—bean sprouts, cabbage, bell peppers, and onions, or use an assorted vegetable medley that you prefer. I'm adding fermented salted black beans, and I think Chinese wood ear mushrooms, although bland in taste, provide excellent textural crunch to the dish. Both fermented salted black beans and wood ear mushrooms can be bought from a Chinese supermarket or online. I promise these will become pantry stir-fry staples.

Serves 2 cal 206 carbs 25.6g protein 5.4g fat 9.2g

Whisk together all the ingredients for the sauce in a small bowl, then set aside.

Heat a wok over high heat until smoking and add the canola oil. Add the ginger and stir-fry for a few seconds, then add the fermented salted black bean mixture and toss for 2 seconds. Next, add the carrot and cook for 1 minute, then add the shiitake mushrooms, wood ear mushrooms, baby corn, and bamboo shoots and stir-fry together for 1 minute.

Add the sauce and bring to a boil. When the sauce has thickened, add the bean sprouts and cook for 30 seconds, then garnish with the scallions. Transfer to a serving plate and serve with jasmine rice.

V Ve DF

Yellow Bean Sesame Bean Sprouts

For the sauce

1 teaspoon Shaoxing rice wine or dry sherry

1 teaspoon whole fermented yellow beans

1 tablespoon vegetarian mushroom sauce (if you can't find this, use hoisin sauce)

1 tablespoon low-sodium light soy sauce

¼ cup cold vegetable stock

1 teaspoon cornstarch

For the stir-fry

1 tablespoon canola oil

1 teaspoon freshly grated ginger

2 scallions, trimmed and finely sliced into rounds

1¼ pounds fresh bean sprouts

1 teaspoon toasted white sesame seeds, to garnish

This dish is quick and simple but full of flavor. The punchy fermented yellow beans transform the beansprouts and the sesame seeds and scallions round it off nicely with a fresh, nutty, aromatic bite. It's great with meat and fish dishes and also alongside stir-fried vegetables. Sometimes simplicity is king.

Serves 4 cal 106 carbs 7.3g protein 3.9g fat 6.4g

Whisk together all the ingredients for the sauce in a small bowl, then set aside.

Heat a wok over high heat until smoking and add the canola oil. Add the ginger and stir-fry for a few seconds, then add the scallions and toss for 5 seconds. Add the bean sprouts, then pour in the sauce and toss over high heat for 30 seconds, ensuring that the sauce coats the bean sprouts well.

Transfer to a serving plate, garnish with the toasted sesame seeds, and serve immediately.

20 mins*

6–7 mins

* includes cooking the rice

Curried Zucchini and Lotus Root Fried Rice

1 tablespoon canola oil

knob of fresh ginger, peeled and grated

1 red cayenne chile, seeded and finely chopped

scallions, trimmed and sliced into ½-inch rounds

¼ teaspoon medium curry powder

7 ounces zucchini, halved lengthwise, then cut into ¼-inch half-moon slices (about 1¾ cups)

1 tablespoon Shaoxing rice wine or dry sherry

5½ ounces lotus root, blanched in hot water, drained and cut into ¼-inch slices

1½ cups cooked basmati rice (¾ cup uncooked)

2 tablespoons low-sodium light soy sauce

1 teaspoon toasted sesame oil

2 pinches of cracked black pepper

I love this combination of sweet zucchini and crunchy lotus roots. If you can't get lotus root, substitute canned water chestnuts—they work just as well. Satisfying, tasty, and healthy!

Serves 2 cal 314 carbs 52.9g protein 8.9g fat 8.8g

Heat a wok over high heat until smoking and add the canola oil. Add the ginger, chopped chile, and scallions and explode the flavors in the wok for a few seconds.

Add the curry powder followed by the zucchini, then toss for 30 seconds and season with the Shaoxing rice wine or dry sherry. Add the lotus root pieces and toss for 30 seconds, then add the cooked rice and toss for 3 minutes so that all the flavors are incorporated.

Season with the light soy sauce, toasted sesame oil, and cracked black pepper and serve.

Spicy Saucy Sichuan Mushroom Chow Mein

For the Sichuan spicy sauce
½ cup cold water
1 tablespoon chili bean paste
2 tablespoons Chinkiang black
   rice vinegar or balsamic
   vinegar
1 tablespoon low-sodium light
   soy sauce
1 teaspoon brown sugar
1 tablespoon cornstarch
1 teaspoon toasted sesame oil

For the stir-fry
1 tablespoon canola oil
2 small garlic cloves, crushed and
   coarsely chopped
1-inch piece of fresh ginger,
   peeled and finely grated
1 large red cayenne chile, seeded
   and sliced
7 ounces oyster mushrooms
4 ounces baby bok choy, leaves
   separated
1 tablespoon Shaoxing rice wine
   or dry sherry
1¾ cups cooked Chinese
   egg noodles (5½ ounces
   uncooked)

A quick midweek supper that's delicious, simple, and packs a punch. I love using oyster mushrooms, but you can use whichever mushrooms you prefer.

Serves 2 cal 404 carbs 62.8g protein 11g fat 12.6g

Whisk together all the ingredients for the Sichuan spicy sauce in a small bowl, then set aside.

Heat a wok over high heat until smoking, then add the canola oil. Add the garlic, ginger, and chile and stir-fry for a few seconds. Add the mushrooms and cook for 1 minute, then add the bok choy leaves and Shaoxing rice wine or dry sherry and toss for another minute.

Add the spicy sauce and bring to a boil. Add the cooked egg noodles and toss together until the sauce coats all the noodles and the noodles are warmed through. Serve immediately.

10 mins*

5 mins

* includes cooking the noodles

V **DF**

Hoisin Snow Pea and Cashew Chow Mein

For the noodles

1¾ cups cooked Chinese egg noodles (5½ ounces dried noodles)

1 teaspoon toasted sesame oil

For the stir-fry

1 tablespoon canola oil

knob of fresh ginger, peeled and grated

2 cups snow peas, sliced in half if large

2 cups sugar snap peas

pinch of Chinese five-spice powder

¼ cup cold vegetable stock

1 tablespoon hoisin sauce

2 tablespoons low-sodium light soy sauce

pinch of light brown sugar

2 tablespoons roasted cashews

Here the crunchy snow peas, sugar snap peas, and cashews contrast beautifully with the Chinese egg noodles. Perfect for a quick midweek supper.

Serves 2 cal 444 carbs 58.4g protein 15.5g fat 17.4g

If using dried noodles, cook according to the package instructions. Drain and refresh under cold water, then drizzle with the toasted sesame oil and set aside.

Heat a wok over high heat until smoking and add the canola oil. Add the ginger and stir-fry for 5 seconds, then add the snow peas and sugar snap peas. Toss for 1 minute, then season with a pinch of five-spice powder.

Add the vegetable stock, followed by the cooked noodles, and toss for 1 minute. Season with the hoisin, light soy sauce, and light brown sugar, then add the cashews and toss together for 1 minute.

Transfer to a serving plate and serve immediately.

V Ve DF

Vegetable Chop Suey

For the sauce
½ cup cold vegetable stock
1 tablespoon low-sodium light
    soy sauce
1 teaspoon rice vinegar
pinch of brown sugar
1 tablespoon cornstarch

For the stir-fry
1 tablespoon canola oil
2 garlic cloves, finely chopped
½ white onion, cut into half-
    moon slices
1 medium carrot, cut into 1-inch x
    ½-inch rectangular slices
4 large fresh shiitake
    mushrooms, sliced
6 ounces broccolini, sliced
    diagonally into 1-inch pieces
1 tablespoon Shaoxing rice wine
    or dry sherry
1 x 8-ounce can sliced water
    chestnuts, drained
a large handful of bean sprouts
2 scallions, trimmed and cut
    diagonally into 1-inch slices

In Chinese this dish is called *Za Tsui*, which means "chopped pieces," which can mean vegetables as well as slithers of shrimp, pork, chicken, or tofu, and is often made up of leftovers. Essentially, anything goes. It dates from the nineteenth-century Gold Rush in the US when Chinese immigrants, brought over to work on the American railroad, would cook whatever was available, often together with Egg Foo Yung (see page 101). It's humble but so satisfying that it is still popular to this day. Serve with steamed jasmine rice, or you can toss in cooked Chinese egg noodles for a spicy chow mein.

Serves 2 cal 197 carbs 25.7g protein 6.8g fat 8g

Whisk together all the ingredients for the sauce in a bowl, then set aside.

Heat a wok over high heat until smoking and add the canola oil. Add the garlic and white onion and stir-fry for 10 seconds to release their aroma. Add the carrot and toss for 2 minutes until softened, then add the shiitake mushrooms and broccolini and toss over high heat for 30 seconds.

Season with the Shaoxing rice wine or dry sherry, then add the water chestnuts, bean sprouts, and scallions. Pour in the sauce and bring to a boil, coating the ingredients well.

Transfer to a serving dish and serve immediately with rice or noodles.

15
mins*

5–6
mins

* includes soaking time

V   DF

1¾ cups cooked Chinese
  egg noodles (5½ ounces
  uncooked)
1 teaspoon toasted sesame oil
1 tablespoon canola oil
pinch of sea salt flakes
1 tablespoon freshly grated
  ginger
3 garlic cloves, finely chopped
7 ounces asparagus spears, cut
  into 2-inch slices
1 tablespoon Shaoxing rice wine
  or dry sherry
1 ounce dried wood ear
  mushrooms, soaked in hot
  water for 15 minutes, drained,
  and cut into 1-inch "wavy"
  pieces
¼ cup vegetable stock
1 tablespoon potato flour
  blended with 1 tablespoon
  cold water
1 teaspoon low-sodium light soy
  sauce
½ teaspoon toasted sesame oil
small handful of roasted cashews

Asparagus, Wood Ear Mushrooms, and Cashews in Ginger Garlic Sauce

This makes a delicious meal in minutes—nothing beats fresh asparagus in a sticky, saucy stir-fry. However, be prepared to move fast and read the recipe through prior to cooking so the process is in your head before you start. You won't have time to stop and chop, let alone stop and read. And don't forget to finish with a crunch of your choice, I love roasted cashews.

Serves 2 cal 495 carbs 66.7g protein 14.1g fat 19.7g

Cook the noodles according to the package instructions, then rinse under the cold tap, drain, and drizzle with the sesame oil.

Heat a wok over high heat until smoking, then add the canola oil, and give the oil a swirl. Add the sea salt and let it dissolve in the hot oil. Add the ginger and garlic in quick succession and stir-fry for a few seconds, then add the asparagus and stir-fry for less than 1 minute. Add the Shaoxing rice wine around the rim of the wok to create steam and cook until it has all evaporated.

Add the wood ear mushrooms and toss together for another minute, then add the vegetable stock. Bring the liquid to a boil, then stir in the blended potato flour—this helps bind the sauce to the ingredients. Season with the soy sauce and add a drop of sesame oil, then toss in the cashews—all in one swoop. Add the cooked egg noodles and stir-fry for 30 seconds to heat through. Give everything a final stir, then serve.

CHING'S TIP
Please read the recipe through prior to cooking so the process is in your head before you start, as you won't have time to stop and chop, or even stop and read.
Keep the wok on the highest heat at all times; if it gets too hot, move it away from the heat source. If it's not hot enough, bring it back to the heat. If ingredients start to burn, add a small splash of water to reduce the heat and prevent them from burning further.

Vegetarian Tofu-style Lionhead "Meatballs"

For the "meatballs"

10 ounces fresh firm tofu, drained

1 teaspoon freshly grated ginger

1 teaspoon fresh cilantro stems

1 scallion, finely chopped

1 teaspoon Shaoxing rice wine or dry sherry

½ teaspoon toasted sesame oil

pinch of sea salt flakes

pinch of ground white pepper

1 large egg, lightly beaten

⅓ cup cornstarch

2 cups peanut oil

2 large scallions, cut on a diagonal into ½-inch pieces, to garnish

For the soup stock and noodles

3 cups vegetable stock

4 ounces Chinese cabbage, sliced lengthwise into strips 1¼-inch wide

3 fresh shiitake mushrooms, sliced

½ cup mung bean noodles

1 tablespoon low-sodium light soy sauce

pinch of sea salt flakes

pinch of ground white pepper

1 tablespoon cornstarch blended with 2 tablespoons cold water (optional)

Lionhead Meatballs is a dish that originates from Shanghai and is said to have been something the emperor ate. The meatballs are usually made of pork and first deep-fried, then braised and served in a light broth of Chinese leaves, curled around each meatball to resemble the "mane" of a lion. For my vegetarian version I've substituted mashed tofu for ground pork, but the seasoning ingredients are the same as for the traditional meatballs. You can serve them in broth, with rice, or add mung bean noodles, as I have here.

Serves 2 cal 665 carbs 85.8g protein 21g fat 27.9g

To make the meatballs, put the tofu in a large bowl and mash with a fork. Add all the remaining "meatball" ingredients up to the egg and stir to combine. Using wetted hands, shape the mixture into 12 medium golf ball shapes, then dust with the cornstarch and place on a plate.

Heat a wok over high heat until smoking and add the peanut oil. Using a spider or metal spoon, carefully lower each meatball into the oil and spoon some of the oil over the meatballs to brown them. When the meatballs have turned golden brown, remove carefully and place on a heatproof plate lined with paper towels. For a crisper meatball, you can deep-fry them twice by reheating the oil and repeating the process.

Pour the oil out of the wok into a heatproof bowl, leaving 1 tablespoon, and pour in the stock. Add the cabbage, mushrooms, mung bean noodles, and soy sauce and bring to a boil. Cook over medium heat for 6 to 7 minutes until the noodles are cooked through and translucent and the cabbage has wilted. Season to taste with salt and white pepper. Stir in the blended cornstarch for a silky texture to the broth.

Ladle the broth and noodles into a serving bowl, add the tofu balls, and sprinkle with the scallions. Serve immediately.

V DF

Honey Miso Broccoli and Cauliflower

For the sauce
1 tablespoon red miso paste
1 teaspoon peeled and grated
    fresh ginger
1 tablespoon honey
pinch of shimichi pepper flakes
    (optional)
1 tablespoon tamari
3 tablespoons mirin

For the stir-fry
1 tablespoon canola oil
1 small scallion, sliced
¼ head broccoli, separated into
    florets, stalks cut diagonally
    into ¼-inch slices
    (about 1¾ cups)
¼ head cauliflower, separated
    into florets, stalks cut
    diagonally into ¼-inch slices
    (about 1¾ cups)
toasted pumpkin seeds
    (optional)

I love the sweet-salty combination of honey and miso; it's delicious with vegetables and even popular with children who think they don't like broccoli. Easy and simple and extremely healthy when served like this with pumpkin seeds and brown rice.

Serves 2 cal 223 carbs 26.9g protein 7.9g fat 9.1g

Whisk together all the ingredients for the sauce in a bowl, then set aside.

Heat a wok over high heat until smoking and add the canola oil. Add the scallions and stir-fry for a few seconds to release their aroma. Add the broccoli and cauliflower and toss for 1 minute. Drizzle in ½ cup cold water around the edge of the wok to create some steam to help cook the vegetables.

Give the sauce a stir, then add to the wok and toss over high heat, ensuring all the vegetables are coated in the sauce. Cook for 1 minute.

Garnish with the pumpkin seeds (if using) and transfer to a serving plate. Serve with steamed brown rice.

V Ve DF

Spring Pointed Cabbage with Corn and Chile

2 tablespoons canola oil

2 garlic cloves, crushed and finely chopped

1-inch piece of fresh ginger, peeled and grated

1 small cayenne chile, seeded and finely chopped

10 ounces spring pointed cabbage leaves, sliced into 1-inch pieces

kernels from 2 whole fresh ears of corn

2 tablespoons Shaoxing rice wine or dry sherry

¼ cup vegetable stock

2 tablespoons low-sodium light soy sauce

1 teaspoon cornstarch blended with 1 tablespoon cold water

1 teaspoon toasted sesame oil

1 large scallion, finely sliced (optional)

The hot chile and umami soy perfectly balance out the sweetness of the cabbage leaves and crunchy corn kernels. Perfect with steamed rice for a light, healthy supper.

Serves 2 cal 263 carbs 23.3g protein 9.2g fat 15.4g

Heat a wok over high heat until smoking and add the canola oil. Swirl the oil in the wok, then add the garlic, ginger, and cayenne chile very quickly and stir-fry for a few seconds. Add the cabbage leaves and cook for 1 minute, tossing them in the wok until seared and starting to wilt. Add the corn kernels and toss for 1 minute, then season with the Shaoxing rice wine or dry sherry and cook until evaporated.

Add the vegetable stock and season with the light soy sauce, then bring any liquid in the wok to a simmer. Pour in the blended cornstarch and toss to mix well, then season with the toasted sesame oil.

Garnish with the sliced scallions and serve immediately.

General Tso's Tofu

14 ounces fresh firm tofu,
     drained and cut into 1-inch
     cubes
¼ cup potato flour or cornstarch
peanut oil for deep-frying
1 large egg, lightly beaten
1 garlic clove, crushed but left
     whole
4 whole dried Sichuan chiles
1 medium white onion, cut into
     1-inch squares
1 large red bell pepper, seeded
     and cut into 1-inch squares
1 tablespoon Shaoxing rice wine
     or dry sherry
4 scallions, chopped into 1-inch
     pieces

For the sauce
1 tablespoon yellow bean sauce
2 tablespoons low-sodium light
     soy sauce
1 tablespoon tomato paste
1 tablespoon rice vinegar or cider
     vinegar
1 tablespoon chili sauce
1 teaspoon light brown sugar or
     honey
1 teaspoon dark soy sauce

For the garnish and to serve
½ cup peanuts, toasted and
     chopped (optional)
handful of toasted sesame seeds

Variations of this recipe are found all over the world. It was invented by a Hunanese chef named Peng-Chang Kuei, who cooked at state banquets and official events for the Chinese Nationalist party and fled with them to Taiwan during the Second World War, where he came up with the dish in the 1950s. Its original flavors were Hunanese—hot, sour, salty, and heavy—but when he moved to New York in 1973 he made it sweeter to suit the American palate. The original dish used chicken but I like it with crunchy fried tofu. If you don't like frying the tofu, use smoked firm tofu and follow the rest of the recipe. Serve with steamed jasmine rice and broccoli.

Serves 2 kcal 914 carbs 52.9g protein 37.5g fat 61.9g

Whisk together all the ingredients for the sauce in a bowl, then set aside.

Coat the tofu cubes in the potato flour or cornstarch and place on a plate. Heat a wok over high heat and fill to a quarter of its depth with peanut oil. Heat the oil to 350ºF or until a piece of bread dropped in turns golden brown in 15 seconds. Coat each piece of tofu in the beaten egg and, using a spider or slotted metal spoon, lower into the wok. Cook for about 5 minutes until all the tofu is golden brown, then remove and place on a plate lined with paper towels to drain any excess oil.

Leave 1 tablespoon oil in the wok and strain the rest through a sieve into a heatproof bowl. Heat the wok over high heat and when it starts to smoke, add the garlic and dried chiles and fry for a few seconds to release their aroma. Add the white onion and stir-fry for 1 minute, then add the red bell pepper and Shaoxing rice wine or dry sherry and cook until the sauce has reduced and has a slightly sticky consistency. Toss in the fried tofu pieces and add the scallions.

Transfer to a serving plate and garnish with the peanuts and sesame seeds.

*** includes marinating
the mock duck**

V Ve DF

Five-spice Mock Duck and Seasonal Greens

10 ounces canned mock duck, drained and cut into ½-inch strips

1 scallion, finely sliced

For the marinade

1 garlic clove, finely chopped

1 teaspoon Chinese five-spice powder

1 teaspoon dark soy sauce

pinch of sea salt

pinch of ground white pepper

For the stir-fry

1 tablespoon canola oil

2 whole dried chiles, torn

1 tablespoon Shaoxing rice wine or dry sherry

2 ounces broccolini, sliced diagonally into 1-inch pieces (about ½ cup)

2 ounces haricots verts, sliced diagonally into 1-inch pieces (about ½ cup)

1 tablespoon cornstarch blended with 2 tablespoons cold water

Mock duck is made from wheat gluten and gives a meaty texture, "mocking" meat. It is used in a lot of Buddhist vegetarian dishes within Chinese cuisine. It comes in cans, which can be found in many Chinese supermarkets. If you can't find it, use meaty portobello mushrooms or smoked tofu. For meat lovers, a tender sirloin steak or chicken thighs sliced into strips work well—just dust the strips with cornstarch after marinating to seal in the meat juices before frying. Enjoy!

Serves 2 cal 253 carbs 18.9g protein 21.1g fat 11.1g

First, marinate the tofu: Place all the ingredients for the marinade in a small bowl or plastic bag, add the mock duck, and marinate for 20 minutes.

Heat a wok over high heat until smoking and add the canola oil, then add the dried chiles and toss for 10 seconds to release their aroma. Add the marinated mock duck pieces and toss for 30 seconds. Season with the Shaoxing rice wine or dry sherry and cook until evaporated.

Add the broccoli and green beans and toss for 1 minute until tender and the vegetables turn a deeper opaque green. Add ½ cup cold water and bring to a simmer, then stir in the blended cornstarch to thicken the sauce. Garnish with the scallions and serve immediately.

V Ve DF

King Trumpet Mushrooms with Chives

1 tablespoon canola oil

knob of fresh ginger, peeled and grated

10 ounces King Trumpet mushrooms, sliced into ½-inch coins

1 to 2 tablespoons Shaoxing rice wine or dry sherry

1 tablespoon oyster sauce or mushroom sauce

1 tablespoon low-sodium light soy sauce

pinch of ground black pepper

2 tablespoons chives, finely chopped, to garnish

If you are a fan of Beef in Oyster Sauce but looking for a veggie alternative, then this is the dish for you. King Trumpet mushrooms are meaty in texture and the perfect accompaniment to a rich oyster sauce. This is simple, easy, and delicious. Perfect served with steamed seasonal greens and some steamed jasmine rice.

Serves 2 cal 76 carbs 3.4g protein 2.3g fat 5.9g

Heat a wok over high heat until smoking and add the canola oil. Add the ginger and stir-fry for a few seconds to release its aroma, then add the King Trumpet pieces and toss for 30 seconds to sear the mushrooms.

Add the Shaoxing rice wine or dry sherry and cook until evaporated. Season with the oyster or mushroom sauce, the light soy sauce, and a pinch of ground black pepper.

Garnish with the chopped chives and serve immediately.

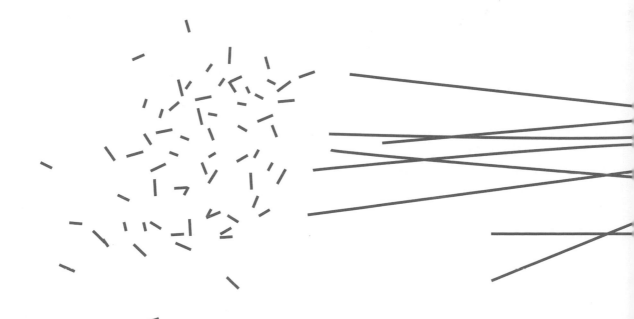

V Ve DF

Eggplant in a Spicy Peanut Sauce

For the sauce

1 teaspoon smooth peanut butter

1 tablespoon chili bean paste

1 teaspoon sesame paste, such as tahini

2 tablespoons low-sodium light soy sauce

1 tablespoon Chinkiang black rice vinegar or balsamic vinegar

1 tablespoon cornstarch

¼ cup cold water

For the stir-fry

1 tablespoon canola oil, plus 1 teaspoon

10 ounces purple eggplant, sliced into ½-inch x 1-inch strips

1 red chile, seeded and finely sliced

1 tablespoon Shaoxing rice wine or dry sherry

For the garnish

1 scallion, finely sliced

1 teaspoon toasted sesame seeds

I love Sichuan-style Fish Fragrant Eggplant, which is a spicy, pungent, and salty dish, but I always feel it's missing a nutty sesame flavor. The addition of peanut butter and tahini takes this dish to another level—the perfect comfort dish. Serve with wheat noodles or steamed jasmine rice.

Serves 2   cal 192   carbs 18.2g   protein 4g   fat 11.8g

Whisk together all the ingredients for the sauce in a small bowl, then set aside.

Heat a wok over high heat until smoking and add 1 tablespoon canola oil. Add the eggplant strips and stir-fry for 4 to 5 minutes, while adding ½ cup of water in drops to soften the eggplant. Once softened, push the eggplant to one side of the wok and add 1 teaspoon canola oil. Add the sliced chile to the oil and cook for a few seconds, then season with the Shaoxing rice wine or dry sherry.

Give the sauce a stir, then add to the eggplant and cook gently, stirring and tossing all the ingredients together until the sauce is heated through and has coated the eggplant—about 2 minutes.

Garnish with the scallion and toasted sesame seeds and serve immediately with some jasmine rice or noodles.

Chili Bean Tofu with Enoki Mushrooms and Bok Choy

1 tablespoon canola oil

2 small shallots, finely chopped

12 ounces fresh firm tofu, drained and cut into ¾-inch cubes

1 tablespoon Shaoxing rice wine or dry sherry

7 ounces baby bok choy, halved

4 ounces fresh enoki mushrooms, stalks trimmed

For the sauce

½ cup cold vegetable stock

1 tablespoon chili bean paste

1 tablespoon low-sodium light soy sauce

½ teaspoon dark soy sauce

pinch of light brown sugar

1 teaspoon cornstarch

For the garnish

teaspoon chili oil

handful of fresh cilantro, coarsely chopped

Stewed dishes are, in my opinion, perfect winter food. The tofu carries the spicy notes of the chili bean paste and the seasonings in this dish so well. The enoki provide a stringy, sweet, soft texture while the bok choy brings a fresh peppery note to the dish. Perfect served with steamed jasmine rice or rice noodles.

Serves 2 cal 276 carbs 13g protein 20.1g fat 15.3g

Whisk together all the ingredients for the sauce in a bowl, then set aside.

Heat a wok over high heat until it starts to smoke, then add half the canola oil. Stir-fry the shallots for 1 minute, then add the tofu cubes. Let the tofu sear and brown for 10 seconds on one side, then flip over. Add the Shaoxing rice wine or dry sherry and the bok choy leaves and toss together gently for 2 minutes to wilt the leaves.

Give the sauce a stir, then pour into the wok and bring to a boil. Add the enoki mushrooms and stir in to wilt.

Transfer to a serving plate, garnish with the chili oil and chopped cilantro, and serve.

* includes soaking the rice noodles

V DF

Vegetarian Char Kway Teow

1 tablespoon canola oil

2 garlic cloves, finely chopped

2 small shallots, sliced

1 red cayenne chile, seeded and finely chopped

6 ounces fried tofu, sliced into strips ½-inch wide x 1-inch in length

½ teaspoon medium curry powder

1 tablespoon Shaoxing rice wine

14 ounces Thai or wide rice noodles, soaked in warm water for 5 minutes, then drained

pinch of superfine sugar

2 tablespoons low-sodium light soy sauce

2 large organic eggs, lightly beaten

1½ cups fresh bean sprouts

2 scallions, sliced diagonally into 1-inch pieces

For the garnish

1 red chile, finely chopped, dressed in 1 tablespoon low-sodium light soy sauce

2 tablespoons fried crispy garlic shallots

Char Kway Teow is one of my favorite wok-fried noodles. I think the best I have tried have been in Malaysia in Penang and Ipoh at the many street hawker stalls. This is my version; it comes originally from Chazhou in China and there are many different versions. I like mine with fried tofu but you can use shrimp or slices of pork too.

The trick is to use a small hint of medium curry powder for a warming spice note, and while Shaoxing rice wine is not a traditional ingredient, it imparts a sweet note. You can buy ready-to-eat wide rice noodles from most supermarkets, so this will be quick and easy to cook.

Serves 2 cal 649 carbs 70.5g protein 31.3g fat 27.7g

Heat a wok over high heat until smoking and add the canola oil. Add the garlic, shallots, and chile and stir-fry for a few seconds to release their aroma. Add the fried tofu and curry powder and toss until all the tofu has turned crispy and golden yellow. Season with the Shaoxing rice wine or dry sherry, then add the noodles and toss for 2 minutes. Add 1 pinch of superfine sugar and the light soy sauce and ensure all the ingredients are covered in the seasoning.

Make a well in the center of the mixture, pour in the beaten eggs and let settle for a few seconds, and then cook for 30 seconds, stirring and mixing the egg to combine with the noodles. Add the bean sprouts and scallions and toss together for 30 seconds until the bean sprouts have wilted slightly.

Transfer to a serving plate. Garnish with the finely chopped chile dressed in soy sauce and sprinkle with the crispy fried garlic shallots. Serve immediately.

* includes soaking time for the mushrooms and noodles

V Ve DF

Quick Cauliflower, Cabbage, Tofu, and Spinach Casserole with Glass Noodles

1 tablespoon canola oil

knob of fresh ginger, peeled and cut into thick coin slices

2 small shallots, finely sliced

1 medium red chile, seeded and finely chopped

6 dried Chinese mushrooms, soaked in warm water for 20 minutes, drained, and sliced, stalks intact

½ teaspoon dark soy sauce

1 tablespoon Shaoxing rice wine or dry sherry

½ head Chinese cabbage, such as Napa, sliced lengthwise into thirds

4¼ cups hot vegetable stock

1 cup cauliflower florets, washed

12 ounces fresh firm tofu, sliced into ½-inch cubes

3½ ounces dried mung bean noodles, rehydrated in hot water for 5 minutes, then drained

1 to 2 tablespoons low-sodium light soy sauce

1 tablespoon Chinkiang black rice vinegar or balsamic vinegar

pinch of ground white pepper

pinch of sea salt

small handful of fresh spinach leaves

For the garnish

1 teaspoon chili oil

handful of fresh cilantro leaves

Casseroles imply a really lengthy cooking time, but I promise this dish won't take hours. The cauliflower and cabbage leaves quickly soften to impart a delicate sweetness, the tofu absorbs all the umami richness in the broth, and the mung bean noodles provide a slippery bite. It's addictive and yet light and delicious and so perfect for those in between hot and cold days when you want something nutritious.

Serves 4 cal 249 carbs 31.8g protein 11.7g fat 8.8g

Heat a wok over high heat until smoking and add the canola oil. Add the ginger, shallots, chile, and mushrooms and toss for 30 seconds to release their aroma. Season with the dark soy sauce and toss for a few more seconds, then add the Shaoxing rice wine or dry sherry.

Add the cabbage then pour in the hot vegetable stock. Add the cauliflower, tofu pieces, and mung bean noodles and season with the light soy sauce to taste. Bring to a boil and cook for 4 minutes. Season with the vinegar, ground white pepper, and salt to taste. Stir in the spinach and let it wilt.

Transfer to large noodle bowls, garnish with the chili oil and fresh cilantro, and serve immediately.

V Ve DF

Fish Fragrant Okra

For the sauce
½ cup cold vegetable stock

1 tablespoon low-sodium light
soy sauce

1 tablespoon Chinkiang black
rice vinegar or balsamic
vinegar

1 tablespoon cornstarch

For the stir-fry
1 tablespoon canola oil

2 garlic cloves, crushed and
finely chopped

1-inch piece of fresh ginger,
peeled and grated

1 medium red chile, seeded and
finely chopped

1 tablespoon chili bean sauce

10 ounces okra, cut into
½-inch slices

1 tablespoon Shaoxing rice wine
or dry sherry

1 scallion, finely sliced

This is an adaptation of Fish Fragrant Eggplant, a classic Sichuan dish that is salty and spicy and perfect with rice. Instead of using Western eggplant or the long purple Asian eggplant, I've decided to try it with okra. In my opinion, the results are superb.

Serves 2 cal 165 carbs 20g protein 5.5g fat 7.5g

Whisk together all the ingredients for the sauce in a bowl, then set aside.

Heat a wok over high heat until smoking and add the canola oil. Add the garlic, ginger, chile, and chili bean sauce and cook for a few seconds. Add the okra and Shaoxing rice wine or dry sherry, then the sauce, and bring to a quick boil. Cook until the sauce has thickened, then stir in the scallion and serve immediately.

V Ve DF

Miso Asparagus with Shimeji

For the sauce
¼ cup hot water

1 teaspoon red miso paste

1 tablespoon low-sodium light
soy sauce

¼ teaspoon brown sugar

For the stir-fry
1 tablespoon canola oil

1 garlic clove, peeled and finely
chopped

1 medium red chile, seeded and
finely chopped

12 tender baby asparagus stalks,
cut diagonally into 1-inch slices

3½ ounces white shimeji
mushrooms, individual stems
separated

3½ ounces brown shimeji
mushrooms, individual stems
separated

I love simple dishes like this one. Miso is a fermented soybean paste that contains good enzymes and bacteria and if you can find an organic red miso bean paste from a Japanese grocer the results will be superb. The miso imparts a rich savory note to the stir-fry, and when mixed with sugar gives a beany salty sweetness to the vegetables. Perfect served with brown rice and Japanese pickles.

Serves 2 cal 94 carbs 4.5g protein 4.6g fat 6.4g

Whisk together all the ingredients for the sauce in a glass measuring cup or bowl, then set aside. Heat a wok over high heat until smoking and add the canola oil.

Add the garlic and chile and stir-fry for a few seconds to release their aroma, then add the baby asparagus and all the shimeji mushrooms. Toss together. Pour in the sauce and simmer for 1 minute until the sauce has thickened and coats the vegetables.

Transfer to a serving plate and serve immediately on its own or with brown rice.

8 mins

6 mins

V Ve DF

Tomato, Green Bell Pepper, Chinese Cabbage, and Scallion

1 tablespoon canola oil

knob of fresh ginger, peeled and grated

2 scallions, finely sliced

4 ripe medium tomatoes, cored and sliced into quarters

1 green bell pepper, seeded and finely chopped

½ Chinese cabbage, leaves separated and cut into 1-inch slices

1 tablespoon Shaoxing rice wine or dry sherry

¼ cup cold vegetable stock

1 tablespoon low-sodium light soy sauce

1 teaspoon rice vinegar or cider vinegar

1 teaspoon cornstarch blended with 1 tablespoon cold water

My grandmother used to make this simple vegetable stir-fry, which contains all the sour, peppery, sweet, pungent, and umami notes that form the basis of Chinese cooking and make it so satisfying. For an additional spicy kick, serve with a side of your favorite chili sauce or chili oil and enjoy.

Serves 2 cal 125 carbs 14.1g protein 3.4g fat 6.4g

Heat a wok over high heat until smoking and add the canola oil. Add the ginger and scallions and stir-fry for a few seconds to release their aroma. Add the tomatoes, green bell pepper, and Chinese cabbage and toss for 3 minutes, until the cabbage starts to wilt and the bell pepper is tender.

Season with the Shaoxing rice wine or dry sherry and the vegetable stock. Stir in the light soy sauce and vinegar, then stir in the blended cornstarch and simmer for a minute or so to thicken the sauce.

Transfer to a serving plate and serve with brown rice.

V DF

Bamboo Shoot Lo Mein

For the Lo Mein sauce
1¼ cups cold vegetable stock

¾ cup cold water

2 tablespoons low-sodium light
soy sauce

1 tablespoon cornstarch

For the stir-fry
9-ounce nest of thin Chinese egg
noodles (2½ cups cooked)

1 tablespoon toasted sesame oil,
plus 1 teaspoon

1 tablespoon canola oil

2 garlic cloves, finely chopped

1 tablespoon freshly grated
ginger

6 large fresh shiitake mushrooms,
sliced, stems discarded

1 x 8-ounce can of bamboo
shoots, drained

7 ounces choy sum, leaves and
stalks cut into 2-inch pieces, or
broccoli florets

1 tablespoon Shaoxing rice wine
or dry sherry

1 teaspoon dark soy sauce

large pinch of ground white
pepper

Lo Mein is a Cantonese dish meaning "stirred noodle." Traditionally, Lo Mein is a variation of wonton noodles where all the components including the noodles are served separately. Lo Mein in Mandarin is known as "Ban Mein"—i.e. mixed sauce noodle, and not necessarily stir-fried together but just tossed together. Don't be fazed by what seems like a long list of ingredients—precook the noodles, combine the ingredients for the sauce, stir-fry the main ingredients, and toss the noodles and ingredients together in the sauce. You can also use whichever type of noodles you prefer, but thin or medium Chinese egg noodles work well.

Serves 2 cal 529 carbs 73.2g protein 14.4g fat 20.5g

Whisk together all the ingredients for the Lo Mein sauce in a bowl, then set aside.

Bring a pot of water to a boil, add the egg noodles, and cook for 3 minutes until al dente. Drain under cold running water, then add 1 teaspoon toasted sesame oil to prevent the noodles from sticking together.

Heat a wok over high heat until smoking and add the canola oil. Add the garlic, ginger, and shiitake mushrooms and toss together for a few seconds, then add the bamboo shoots and stir-fry for less than 1 minute. Add the choy sum and toss together for 1 minute, then pour in the Shaoxing rice wine or dry sherry and the Lo Mein sauce and bring to a boil—1 to 2 minutes. Quickly add the cooked egg noodles and season with the dark soy sauce and 1 tablespoon toasted sesame oil. Stir together well for 1 minute, ensuring all the noodles are coated in the sauce. Season with the ground white pepper.

Transfer to a serving bowl and serve immediately.

CHING'S TIP

If using dried shiitake mushrooms instead of fresh, you can use the water the mushrooms were soaked in instead of the vegetable stock in the sauce.

Red Cooked Shiitake Mushrooms, Pumpkin, and Chestnuts

V Ve DF

14 ounces pumpkin flesh, sliced
    into ½-inch cubes
pinch of salt
1 tablespoon canola oil
1 tablespoon whole five-spice
    with cinnamon bark (the
    cinnamon bark should be
    included in spice mix when
    bought but if not you can add
    1 piece)
10 fresh shiitake mushrooms,
    sliced
1 tablespoon Shaoxing rice wine
    or dry sherry
1 tablespoon low-sodium light
    soy sauce
1 teaspoon dark soy sauce
1 tablespoon brown sugar
10 cooked chestnuts
fresh cilantro leaves, to garnish

Whenever winter draws near, I find myself craving stews and braised dishes and automatically think of spiced chestnuts, pumpkins and earthy shiitake mushrooms. I love the Chinese braised red cooking technique, where dishes are stewed in a soy spiced liquid that imparts a warm red color to the prepared food. It will keep your stomach happy through all the cold months.

Serves 2 cal 224 carbs 35.4g protein 4.9g fat 8.2g

Heat a wok and add 4¼ cups cold water, then bring to a boil and add the pumpkin pieces. Season with salt and boil for 8 minutes until the pumpkin is cooked but still has a bite and retains its cube shape. Spoon out of the wok, drain, and set aside.

Drain the wok and heat over high heat until smoking, then add the canola oil. Swirl the oil around, then add the whole spices and stir-fry for a few seconds, Add the shiitake mushrooms and cook for 30 seconds until fragrant. Add the cooked pumpkin and the Shaoxing rice wine or dry sherry, then cook for 1 minute while stirring.

Add the light and dark soy sauces, pour in ¾ cup of cold water followed by the brown sugar and cooked chestnuts, and bring it all to a boil, gently spooning the liquid over the ingredients. Cook until all the liquid has reduced by half and the ingredients are slightly sticky with the red glaze.

Take off the heat, garnish with some fresh cilantro leaves, and serve immediately.

Vegetarian Thai Eggplant Tom Yum Rice Noodle Soup

1 tablespoon canola oil

1 teaspoon finely grated galangal or ginger

1 stalk of lemongrass, finely sliced

1 whole kaffir lime leaf, fresh or dried

1 red chile, seeded and finely chopped

6 small green baby Thai eggplant, sliced into quarters

1 tablespoon vegetable bouillon powder

2 cups cooked flat wide rice noodles (5½ ounces dried), drizzled with sesame oil

6 ounces fresh, firm tofu, drained and cut into ¾-inch cubes

4 cherry tomatoes

2 small heads of baby bok choy, halved

½ cup reduced fat coconut milk

pinch of brown sugar

1 tablespoon tamari or low-sodium light soy sauce

For the garnish

juice of 1 lime

small handful of Thai basil leaves, sliced into thin ribbons

small handful of fresh cilantro, coarsely chopped

Inspired by the flavors of Thai Hot and Sour Tom Yum Soup, I have made my own version. For Thais, wok-frying all the aromatics is not the correct way to start this recipe, but I love to use the wok to explode the spices in hot oil as I think it injects a slight smoky flavor and enriches the broth. If you can't find Thai eggplant, you can use 7 ounces oyster mushrooms. You can also turn this into a meat or seafood dish and use fish sauce for a salty edge, or adapt it for vegan friends by adding assorted greens. Versatile and delicious.

Serves 2 cal 525 carbs 70g protein 17.9g fat 19.8g

Heat a wok over high heat until smoking and add the canola oil. Add the galangal or ginger, the lemongrass, kaffir lime leaf, and red chile and explode the flavors in the hot oil for 10 seconds to release their aroma. Add the eggplant and toss for 2 minutes (if using oyster mushrooms, cook for 1 minute).

Pour in 3½ cups cold water and season with the vegetable bouillon powder, then cook for 10 minutes over high heat to infuse all the flavors. Once it has come to a boil, add the rice noodles, tofu, cherry tomatoes, and bok choy. Season with the coconut milk, brown sugar, and tamari or soy sauce and bring back to a boil and simmer for a minute.

Transfer to serving bowls and garnish with the lime juice, Thai basil, and fresh cilantro.

Veggie Dan Dan Mein

7 ounces dried wheat noodles
pinch of sea salt
1 teaspoon toasted sesame oil
2 cups hot vegetable stock

For the topping

1 tablespoon peanut oil
2 garlic cloves, finely chopped
1 tablespoon grated ginger
3 red chiles, seeded and finely
    chopped
12-ounce bag Quorn grounds
¾ cup cornichons (or Chinese
    Zha Cai), finely chopped
1 tablespoon Shaoxing rice wine
    or dry sherry
1 tablespoon Chinkiang black rice
    vinegar or balsamic vinegar
1 tablespoon low-sodium light
    soy sauce
1 teaspoon Chinese sesame paste
½ teaspoon ground dry-toasted
    Sichuan peppercorns
freshly ground white pepper

For the chili oil dressing

1 tablespoon chili oil
1 tablespoon toasted sesame oil
1 tablespoon low-sodium light
    soy sauce
pinch of ground dry-toasted
    Sichuan peppercorns
1 red chile, seeded and diced

For the garnish

1 large scallion, finely sliced on
    a diagonal
fresh cilantro leaves

I love using Quorn grounds for this Sichuan dish as it makes it addictive but also light. The peppercorns then give it a lovely numbing zinginess, which I find rather addictive!

Serves 2 cal 678 carbs 85.7g protein 37.2g fat 18.2g

Whisk together all the ingredients for the chili oil dressing in a small bowl and set aside.

Bring a large pot of water to a boil over high heat and add the dried noodles. Season with salt, then stir and cook until al dente—about 4 minutes. Drain, rinse with cold water, shake out any excess liquid, and transfer them to a bowl. Drizzle over the toasted sesame oil and toss to coat well and set aside.

Place the vegetable stock in a saucepan and bring to a gentle simmer. Heat a wok over high heat until smoking and add the peanut oil. Add the garlic, ginger, and chiles and stir-fry for 30 seconds, then add the Quorn grounds and cook for 2 to 3 minutes until browned. Add the cornichons, the Shaoxing rice wine or dry sherry, the vinegar, soy sauce, sesame paste, and ground peppercorns, then stir well until the Quorn takes on the flavorings. Season with ground white pepper and remove from the heat.

To serve, divide the noodles between two large soup bowls, ladle over the topping, and pour the hot stock over the noodles. Garnish with the scallion and cilantro and serve with a spoonful of the chili oil dressing to taste. Serve immediately.

CHING'S TIP
Sesame paste can be substituted with an equal amount of tahini mixed with
1 teaspoon toasted sesame oil.

V Ve DF

Spicy Cilantro Chickpea Fried Rice

1 tablespoon canola oil

2 garlic cloves, crushed and finely chopped

1 small red onion, diced

1 red bell pepper, seeded and diced

1 green bell pepper, seeded and diced

1 x 14-ounce can of chickpeas, drained

1 cup cooked jasmine and wild rice mix

1 tablespoon red wine vinegar

1 tablespoon low-sodium light soy sauce

pinch of dried chile flakes

pinch of sea salt flakes

pinch of ground black pepper

juice of 1 lime

3 tablespoons finely chopped fresh cilantro

This is a pantry fried rice that is perfect for a quick midweek veggie supper. Chickpeas are a high source of protein and I think taste great in this dish together with the tangy vinegar and crunchy peppers.

Serves 2 cal 355 carbs 55.6g protein 13.8g fat 10.2g

Heat a wok and add the canola oil. Stir-fry the garlic and red onion for 1 minute, then add the red and green bell peppers and toss for 30 seconds. Add the chickpeas and rice and toss for 1 minute.

Season with the red wine vinegar, light soy sauce, dried chile flakes, salt, and ground black pepper. Sprinkle with the lime juice, then stir in the finely chopped cilantro and serve immediately.

20 mins*

5 mins

* includes soaking time
for the mushrooms and
noodles

(V) (Ve) (DF)

Japchae—Korean Stir-fried Mixed Vegetable Noodles

There are many versions of this delicious noodle dish the world over but this one is very easy to make at home. I like to use traditional sweet potato starch noodles, which you can buy from a Korean supermarket or online, as they have a great texture and the *gochujang* (Korean chili bean paste), which gives them a delicious smoky spiciness, is my personal addition.

Serves 2 cal 444 carbs 71.5g protein 9g fat 13.7g

For the sauce

1 tablespoon toasted sesame oil

2 tablespoons low-sodium light
soy sauce

1 tablespoon Shaoxing rice wine
or dry sherry

1 teaspoon Korean gochujang
chili paste

1/2 teaspoon sugar

pinch of ground white pepper

For the stir-fry

6 ounces uncooked sweet potato
thread noodles

1 tablespoon canola oil

1 garlic clove, crushed and finely
chopped

1/2 medium white onion, sliced

3 dried Chinese mushrooms,
soaked in hot water for
20 minutes, drained, stalks
discarded, cut into 1/2-inch
slices

1 tablespoon Shaoxing rice wine
or dry sherry

1 medium carrot, sliced into
matchsticks

1 3/4 cups shredded Chinese
cabbage

2 scallions, cut into 1-inch slices

4 ounces baby spinach leaves

1 teaspoon toasted sesame
seeds

Whisk together all the ingredients for the sauce in a small bowl, then set aside.

Cook the noodles in boiling water for 10 minutes. Drain and rinse in cold water, then cut into 5-inch lengths.

Heat a wok over high heat until smoking and add the canola oil. Add the garlic and stir-fry for a few seconds, then add the onion slices and stir-fry over high heat for 10 seconds. Add the mushrooms and toss for 5 seconds, then add the Shaoxing rice wine or dry sherry. Add the carrot, cabbage, and scallions and toss for 30 seconds. Drizzle in the water around the edge of the wok to create steam to help cook the vegetables. Add the spinach and noodles and toss to heat through. Stir in the sauce and cook for 10 seconds.

Remove from the heat and transfer to a serving plate, then garnish with the sesame seeds and serve immediately.

Spicy Potato and Egg Stir-fry

3/4 pound potatoes, peeled

pinch of salt

2 tablespoons canola oil

2 tablespoons finely chopped garlic

knob of fresh ginger, peeled and grated

1 red chile, seeded and finely chopped

1 scallion, finely sliced

2 tablespoons pickled chiles in vinegar

1 teaspoon ground dry-toasted Sichuan peppercorns

2 tablespoons Shaoxing rice wine or dry sherry

pinch of superfine sugar

2 tablespoons chili oil

1 tablespoon toasted white sesame seeds

small handful of fresh cilantro, chopped

For the eggs

3 large organic eggs

1 teaspoon toasted sesame oil

pinch of sea salt flakes

pinch of ground white pepper

The wonderful cook Ms Xingyun Chen, aunt of our friend Jenny Gao, made me a deliciously spicy and crisp potato stir-fry whilst I was filming *Exploring China* with Ken Hom, for the BBC and I've recreated it many times since. I also like to add a little beaten egg that, if you are vegan, you can leave out.

Serves 2 cal 523 carbs 38.3g protein 16.7g fat 34.8g

Cut the potatoes into thin slices, then stack them up and slice into matchstick-size pieces. Soak them in a bowl of cold water with a pinch of salt for 5 minutes. Drain and blot dry with paper towels, then set aside.

Crack the eggs into a bowl, season with the toasted sesame oil, salt, and ground white pepper, and beat lightly to combine.

Heat a wok over high heat until smoking and add the canola oil. Add the garlic, ginger, chile, scallion, pickled chiles, and ground Sichuan peppercorns, then stir-fry for 10 seconds to release their aroma. Add the potato matchsticks and toss for 1 minute until they are coated with all the ingredients. Season with the Shaoxing rice wine or dry sherry and the sugar and toss well to combine.

Make a well in the center of the wok, pour in the beaten egg mixture, and toss together and cook until the eggs are lightly scrambled and still moist. Season with the chili oil and add more salt if necessary. Transfer to a serving plate, garnish with freshly chopped cilantro, and serve immediately.

*** includes cooking
the rice**

V GF DF

Asparagus, Carrot, Shiitake, and Egg White Congee

1 tablespoon canola oil

knob of fresh ginger, peeled and
    grated

2 medium carrots, finely diced
    into 2-inch cubes

¼ teaspoon ground turmeric

½ teaspoon fennel seeds

7 ounces tender asparagus
    spears, cut into 1-inch pieces

small handful of fresh shiitake
    mushrooms, sliced

1½ cups cooked jasmine rice
    (¾ cup uncooked)

1 tablespoon Shaoxing rice wine
    or dry sherry

2½ cups hot vegetable stock

1 to 2 tablespoons tamari

1 teaspoon toasted sesame oil

pinch of ground white pepper

3 large organic egg whites, lightly
    beaten (save the egg yolks for
    an omelet)

1 scallion, finely sliced

**This bowl of congee delivers the perfect nourishing comfort
food. The ginger, fennel, and turmeric spice up the vegetables
and warm the whole body and offer the promise of an instant
lift on a glum day. Vegans can omit the egg and throw in strips
of smoked tofu.**

Serves 2 cal 342 carbs 50.2g protein 15.7g fat 10.5g

Heat a wok over high heat until smoking and add the canola
oil. Add the ginger and carrots and stir-fry for 1 minute. Season
with the turmeric and fennel seeds, then add the asparagus and
mushrooms and continue to cook over high heat to sear the
vegetables.

Tip in the cooked jasmine rice and stir-fry for 1 minute. Add the
Shaoxing rice wine or dry sherry followed by the hot vegetable
stock and bring to a boil, then season to taste with tamari,
sesame oil, and ground white pepper.

Stir in the beaten egg whites and swirl them in the soupy rice to
cook. Ladle out into bowls and sprinkle with the scallion.

V DF

Chinese Wok-fried Spicy Scallion Salsa Verde with Kale and Egg Noodles

1½ cups sliced curly kale

7 ounces dried Chinese egg noodles

1 teaspoon toasted sesame oil

2 tablespoons canola oil

pinch of salt

knob of fresh ginger, peeled and grated

1 red chile, seeded and finely chopped

1 pinch of dried chile flakes

2 scallions, finely chopped

¼ cup cold vegetable stock

1 tablespoon low-sodium light soy sauce

In Chinese cuisine there is a ginger scallion sauce that is normally dressed over steamed chicken, which I adore. I love to use this sauce for a veggie chow mein—its simple and just divine.

Serves 2 cal 482 carbs 75.6g protein 14.9g fat 15.7g

Pour 4¼ cups cold water into a pan and bring to a boil. Add the kale and blanch for 30 seconds, then drain and remove. Cook the noodles according to the package instructions, then run them under the cold tap, drain, and drizzle with the toasted sesame oil.

Heat a wok over high heat until smoking and add the canola oil. Add the salt and let it dissolve in the hot oil, then add the ginger, fresh chile, dried chile, and scallions in quick succession to explode their flavors in the wok.

Add the vegetable stock and stir-fry over medium heat for 30 seconds. Add the kale and cooked egg noodles and toss all the ingredients well to warm through. Season with the light soy sauce and give it one final toss, then transfer to serving plates and eat immediately.

Taiwanese Veggie Dan Zai Noodles

For the noodles
1³⁄₄ cups cooked Chinese egg noodles (5¹⁄₂ ounces dried)
1 teaspoon toasted sesame oil

For the stir-fry
1 tablespoon canola oil
1 small garlic clove, grated
2 small shallots, finely chopped
1¹⁄₂ cups Quorn grounds
1 teaspoon dark soy sauce
2 ounces Chinese cabbage, leaves and stalks separated, cut into ¹⁄₂-inch slices
1 tablespoon Shaoxing rice wine or dry sherry
¹⁄₄ cup vegetable stock
2 tablespoons low-sodium light soy sauce
1 teaspoon toasted sesame oil

For the garnish
1 ounce Chinese chive flowers chopped into 1¹⁄₂-inch pieces or 1-inch scallion
handful of bean sprouts
1 teaspoon toasted sesame oil
1 small garlic clove, minced

This is based on a famous street market dish in Taiwan called *Dan Zai Mein*. Traditionally, ground pork and shrimp head juices are used to create a delicious stock for a souplike dish. My version is vegetarian and uses just the cooking juices from the wok, but it's equally addictive and delicious.

Serves 2 cal 464 carbs 52.5g protein 22.1g fat 17.8g

If using dried egg noodles, cook the noodles in boiling water for 3 minutes. Drain and refresh in cold water. Drizzle the noodles with the toasted sesame oil and put to one side.

Heat a wok over high heat until smoking and add the canola oil, then stir-fry the garlic and shallots for less than 1 minute. Add the Quorn grounds and toss for 1 minute until brown and caramelized. Season with the dark soy sauce, then add the cabbage leaves and stalks and stir-fry for 1 minute. Add the Shaoxing rice wine or dry sherry and cook until evaporated. Add the vegetable stock and cook for 2 minutes until the cabbage has wilted, then season with the light soy sauce. Stir-fry all the ingredients until brown and slightly caramelized, then season with the toasted sesame oil. Keep over low heat.

Pour 4¹⁄₄ cups cold water into a medium pan, bring to a boil, and blanch the Chinese chive flowers and bean sprouts for 10 seconds, then remove and drain. Drizzle with the toasted sesame oil to prevent them from sticking together.

Ladle the Quorn and cabbage mixture into a large serving bowl. Place some noodles on top and ladle over more of the mixture. Place some of the chives and bean sprouts on the side, then garnish with the minced garlic. Serve immediately.

* includes cooking the rice

Egg, Asparagus, Corn, and Shiitake Mushroom Fried Rice

For the scrambled egg

3 large eggs, lightly beaten

pinch of sea salt

pinch of ground white pepper

1 tablespoon canola oil

For the fried rice

1 tablespoon canola oil

2 garlic cloves, finely chopped

4 ounces baby asparagus spears, sliced into ½-inch rounds, tips cut into ¾-inch slices (about 1 cup)

kernels from 1 fresh ear of corn

3 ounces fresh shiitake mushrooms, stems separated, thinly sliced (about 1 cup)

2 cups cooked cold jasmine rice (1 cup uncooked)

2 tablespoons low-sodium light soy sauce

1 teaspoon toasted sesame oil

¼ teaspoon ground white pepper

1 red chile, seeded and finely chopped, to garnish

I love fried rice—the perfect balance between comfort food and healthy food—and especially this combination of asparagus rounds and fresh shiitake mushrooms. I've worked with revered wok masters in Hong Kong who scramble the egg first to get fluffy pieces of egg within the rice dish and so I've used this technique here. This flavorful light dish will make the perfect accompaniment to many of your favorite Chinese dishes or it would be perfect as a meal on its own with a good side of chili sauce.

Serves 2 cal 529 carbs 68.2g protein 19.2g fat 21.8g

Lightly beat the eggs in a bowl and season with sea salt and ground white pepper.

Heat a wok over medium heat and add the canola oil. Pour in the beaten eggs and stir to lightly scramble. When the egg has turned golden and is still fluffy, take off the heat, transfer the eggs to a bowl, and set to one side.

To cook the rice, reheat the wok over high heat and when it starts to smoke, add the canola oil. Add the garlic and stir quickly for a few seconds, then add the asparagus and corn and cook over high heat for 2 minutes until the asparagus starts to turn a deeper green and the corn a golden yellow. Add the mushrooms and toss together, then add the cooked rice. Stir well and toss to combine all the ingredients, then cook for 1 to 2 minutes. Season with the light soy sauce, stir, and mix well.

Return the scrambled eggs to the wok, season with the toasted sesame oil and ground white pepper, and give it a few more stirs.

Remove from the wok, transfer to a large serving plate, and garnish with the chopped chile. Serve immediately.

*includes cooking
the noodles

V DF

Leek, Shiitake, and Bean Sprouts on Thin Egg Noodles

1 tablespoon canola oil

4 ounces baby leeks, sliced on an angle into 1-inch pieces (about 1 cup)

3½ ounces dried Chinese mushrooms, soaked in warm water for 20 minutes, drained, stalks discarded, and cut into ½-inch slices

½ teaspoon dark soy sauce

1 tablespoon Shaoxing rice wine or dry sherry

1¾ cups cooked thin Chinese egg noodles (5½ ounces dried), drained and dressed with 1 teaspoon toasted sesame oil

1 tablespoon mushroom sauce or oyster sauce

pinch of sugar

2 tablespoons low-sodium light soy sauce

handful of bean sprouts

1 teaspoon toasted sesame oil

1 scallion, finely sliced

This is a simple yet rich-tasting dish. The trick is to find plump dried Chinese mushrooms, which can be bought from a Chinese supermarket, as their earthy umami, meaty flavor contrasts beautifully against the texture of the Chinese egg noodles. Delicious!

Serves 2 cal 511 carbs 79.7g protein 15.3g fat 15.6g

Heat a wok over high heat until smoking and add the canola oil. Add the baby leeks and toss for 30 seconds, then add the rehydrated mushrooms and toss for 10 seconds to release their aroma. Add the dark soy sauce and toss well, then add the Shaoxing rice wine or dry sherry and cook until evaporated.

Add the noodles and toss together well for 30 seconds, then season with the mushroom or oyster sauce, the sugar, and light soy sauce. Add the bean sprouts and gently toss and fold into the dish.

Season with the toasted sesame oil, garnish with the scallion, and serve immediately.

V DF

Egg Foo Yung

For the sauce
½ cup cold vegetable stock
¼ teaspoon dark soy sauce
1 tablespoon low-sodium light
    soy sauce
1 tablespoon cornstarch
1 teaspoon toasted sesame oil

For the mushroom gravy
1 tablespoon canola oil
1 garlic clove, finely chopped
small handful of fresh shiitake
    mushrooms, cut into ½-inch
    slices, stalks discarded
1 tablespoons Shaoxing rice wine
    or dry sherry

For the omelet
1 tablespoon canola oil
1 garlic clove, finely chopped
small handful of bean sprouts
1 medium carrot, grated
5 large eggs, lightly beaten,
    seasoned with a pinch each
    of salt and ground white
    pepper and a dash of toasted
    sesame oil
1 scallion, finely sliced diagonally
    into horse ear shapes
2 large romaine lettuce leaves,
    cut into 1-inch slices, to serve

A humble Chinese omelet made using leftovers and served with soy gravy and rice, Egg Foo Yung is thought to have been invented by Chinese immigrants who came to America in the nineteenth century during the nineteenth century Gold Rush. This is my version. I like to add garlic and fresh shiitake mushrooms to create a rich umami gravy, then carrot, bean sprouts, and scallions, and serve it with a hit of crunchy sliced romaine lettuce leaves. It makes a great light supper with or without rice.

Serves 2 cal 393 carbs 15.3g protein 21.2g fat 27.7g

Whisk together all the ingredients for the sauce in a bowl, then set aside.

Heat a wok over high heat until smoking and add 1 teaspoon canola oil. Add the garlic and stir-fry for a few seconds, then add the shiitake mushrooms. Toss for a few seconds, then add the Shaoxing rice wine or dry sherry.

Pour in the sauce and stir until the sauce has thickened, come to a boil, and is glossy and shiny. Transfer the mushroom gravy to a glass heatproof container, cover with foil, and keep warm in an oven.

Give the wok a quick rinse with water and reheat over high heat to make the omelet. Add 1 tablespoon canola oil, then add the garlic and stir-fry for a few seconds. Add the bean sprouts and carrot and toss for 1 minute. Pour in the seasoned beaten eggs and let settle for a few seconds. Slowly unfurl the sides of the omelet, loosening it with a flat spatula, and cook for another 20 seconds. Sprinkle with the scallion, then flip it over and cook for a few more seconds.

Take off the heat and transfer to a serving plate. Pour the mushroom gravy over the top and garnish with the romaine lettuce leaves in the center for a crunchy freshness.

V DF

Chinese Black Bean Eggs and Zucchini Scramble

1 tablespoon canola oil

1 garlic clove, finely chopped

1 red chile, seeded and finely chopped

1 to 2 medium zucchini, cut into ½-inch slices

1 teaspoon fermented salted black beans, rinsed, crushed, and mixed with 1 tablespoon Shaoxing rice wine or dry sherry

1 tablespoon low-sodium light soy sauce

4 large eggs, lightly beaten, seasoned with a pinch of salt and 1 teaspoon toasted sesame oil

For the garnish

drizzle of Sriracha chili sauce

2 tablespoons fresh cilantro leaves, finely chopped

This is a tribute to my grandmother's farm-style cooking. She would fuse traditional southern Chinese ingredients such as fermented salted black beans with vegetables or eggs to create a delicious meal. Fermented salted black beans can be bought from a Chinese grocer online—they are the next best things to salt! This would make a great breakfast or brunch— add some creamy avocado slices on top of the scramble if you like. I think grandmother would love this dish.

Serves 2 cal 270 carbs 6.4g protein 19.6g fat 18.5g

Heat a wok over high heat until smoking and add the canola oil. Add the garlic and chile and toss for 5 seconds to release their aroma. Add the zucchini and toss over high heat for 1 minute. Add the fermented salted black bean mixture and toss for 2 minutes until the zucchini has softened but still has a crunchy texture. Season with the light soy sauce and toss together well.

Pour in the seasoned beaten eggs and stir to scramble, being careful not to break up the zucchini pieces. Once the scrambled eggs are soft and golden, transfer to a serving plate.

Garnish with Sriracha and cilantro leaves for an aromatic finish.

V DF

Beijing Egg and Tomato Noodle Soup

knob of fresh ginger, peeled and grated

9 ounces medium-size tomatoes, cored and quartered

4 ounces Chinese cabbage such as Napa, cut into ¾-inch slices

5 fresh shiitake mushrooms, rinsed, dried, and cut into ½-inch thick slices

1 tablespoon vegetable bouillon powder

1¾ cup cooked wide flat rice noodles (5½ ounces uncooked)

1 tablespoon low-sodium light soy sauce

pinch of ground white pepper

1 tablespoon toasted sesame oil

1 large egg, beaten

2 scallions, sliced diagonally into ½-inch pieces

Based on a snack recipe from Northern China, this egg and tomato soup would be cooked with *la-mein* (hand-pulled noodles) and served from small stalls for breakfast or as a light supper. It was commonly referred to as "Egg Flower Soup," because the egg swirls created a flowery pattern. Traditional wheatflour noodles or wide flat noodles are perfect for this dish as they have a silky texture.

Serves 2 cal 409 carbs 63.3g protein 11.3g fat 13.1g

Pour 4¼ cups boiling water into a wok. Add the ginger, tomatoes, Chinese cabbage, shiitake mushrooms, and vegetable bouillon powder, then bring to a boil and cook for about 2 minutes to soften the vegetables. Turn the heat to medium. Add the rice noodles, season with the light soy sauce, white pepper, and toasted sesame oil, and stir in.

Take a fork or spoon and make a swirling stirring motion in the broth, then add the beaten egg and continue to swirl the egg in the pan (the egg will cook and make a weblike pattern).

Ladle the soup into two large bowls, garnish with the scallions, and eat immediately.

Fish &
shellfish

Radish in Black Rice Vinegar with Crabmeat and Black Sesame Seeds

1 teaspoon canola oil
10 ounces radish leaves
7 ounces radishes, cut into
  ¼-inch slices (1¾ cups)
1 tablespoon Chinkiang black
  rice vinegar or balsamic
  vinegar
pinch of superfine sugar
7 ounces fresh white crabmeat

For the garnish
1 tablespoon black sesame seeds
pinch of dried chile flakes, to
  garnish

Radishes taste really great when they've been lightly stir-fried as the cooking brings out their sweetness, which in turn perfectly complements the sweetness of the crabmeat. Sesame seeds balance this out with a little nuttiness and the chile flakes add a subtle hint of spice.

Serves 2 cal 213 carbs 9.1g protein 26.2g fat 8g

Heat a wok over high heat until smoking and add the canola oil, then add the radish leaves and sliced radishes. Toss for 10 seconds, then drizzle 2 tablespoons cold water around the edge of the wok to create some steam to help cook the radishes. Season immediately with the vinegar and sugar and toss through.

Spoon onto serving plates, then top with the fresh crabmeat and garnish with the sesame seeds and chile flakes.

25*
mins

5
mins

* includes cooking
the rice

1 tablespoon canola oil, plus
    1 teaspoon
2 garlic cloves, finely chopped
7 ounces white cabbage leaves
    (keep the center stalk for
    vegetable stock), leaves torn
    into bite-sized pieces
1 tablespoon Shaoxing rice wine
    or dry sherry
3 tablespoons vegetable stock
1¾ cups cooked and cooled
    jasmine rice (1 cup uncooked)
7 ounces cooked shrimp
½ cup cooked frozen peas
1 tablespoon low-sodium light
    soy sauce
1 tablespoon oyster sauce
large pinch of freshly ground
    white pepper
1 teaspoon toasted sesame oil

Shrimp and Cabbage Fried Rice

I love to add cabbage to fried rice, as it imparts a sweet crunchiness to the dish and, when paired with wok-fried garlic, it is some kind of wonderful! You can use cooked shrimp for quicker results, but ensure you choose a good-quality variety and move fast once they are added to the wok, as you don't want them to turn rubbery.

Serves 2 cal 435 carbs 66.8g protein 23.7g fat 10g

Heat a wok over high heat until smoking and add 1 tablespoon canola oil. Add the garlic and stir-fry for a few seconds, then add the cabbage and stir-fry for 1 minute over high heat. Season with the Shaoxing rice wine or dry sherry, then add the vegetable stock to create steam to help cook the cabbage. Cook for another minute until the cabbage has softened. (If there is any excess liquid in the wok, pour it into a small bowl and keep to use as a seasoning later if the rice is a little dry.)

Return the wok to the heat, push the cabbage to one side, and add 1 teaspoon canola oil. Add the cooked jasmine rice and fry the rice and cabbage together for 1 minute. Add the cooked shrimp and peas and toss until all the ingredients are thoroughly combined.

Season with the light soy sauce, oyster sauce, ground white pepper, and toasted sesame oil and toss together well. Serve immediately.

Shrimp with Shishito Peppers

2 tablespoons canola oil

pinch of sea salt flakes

1 garlic clove, crushed and finely chopped

1 red chile, seeded and finely chopped

7 ounces shishito peppers, left whole

10 ounces cooked jumbo shrimp

1 tablespoon mirin

2 tablespoons low-sodium light soy sauce

juice of 1 lime

pinch of sugar

This is a delicious spicy dish—I love the heat of shishito peppers, especially not knowing whether the next hit will be sweet and peppery or sweet and POW! It is a bit of a roulette-type situation, so be careful if you are not into spicy food. You can always use green bell pepper strips as a substitute. Enjoy!

Serves 2 cal 254 carbs 11g protein 26.1g fat 11.9g

Heat a wok over high heat until smoking and add the canola oil. Add the salt and let it dissolve in the hot oil. Add the garlic and red chile and toss for a few seconds. Add the shishito peppers, toss for 30 seconds until they are seared on the outside and beginning to soften, then stir-fry for another minute. Add the cooked shrimp and toss for less than 1 minute (or cook raw shrimp for 2 to 3 minutes, depending on their size). Season with the mirin, the light soy sauce, lime juice, and sugar.

Transfer to serving plates and serve on its own as an appetizer, or with jasmine rice as a main meal.

DF

Oyster Sauce Scallops and Snow Peas

1 tablespoon canola oil

knob of fresh ginger, peeled and grated

8 medium-sized scallops

1 tablespoon Shaoxing rice wine or dry sherry

1 cup snow peas, left whole

1 teaspoon oyster sauce

1 tablespoon low-sodium light soy sauce

1 teaspoon toasted sesame oil

The umami oyster sauce is a great partner for the sweet scallops and the snow peas deliver a lovely sweet crunch. Use the freshest scallops you can get hold of and you cannot go wrong.

Serves 2 cal 133 carbs 5.1g protein 10.5g fat 7.5g

Heat a wok over high heat until smoking and add the canola oil. Add the ginger and toss for a few seconds to release its aroma. Add the scallops and cook for 5 seconds until seared and browned, then flip them over. Season with the Shaoxing rice wine or dry sherry, then add the snow peas and stir-fry over high heat for 5 seconds. Add a small splash of water around the edge of the wok to create some steam to help cook the snow peas. Season with the oyster sauce and light soy sauce and toss to coat well. Drizzle in the toasted sesame oil at the end.

Transfer to a serving bowl and serve immediately.

DF

Spicy Honey Garlic Shrimp with Water Chestnuts

1 tablespoon canola oil

2 garlic cloves, crushed and finely chopped

knob of fresh ginger, peeled and grated

1 red chile, seeded and finely chopped

7 ounces raw shrimp, shelled and deveined

1 tablespoon Shaoxing rice wine or dry sherry

1 x 8-ounce can sliced water chestnuts, drained

1 teaspoon chili bean paste

1 tablespoon honey

1 tablespoon low-sodium light soy sauce

2 scallions, cut on an angle into ½-inch slices

This is a quick and easy stir-fry dish, perfect for when you need dinner on the table in minutes. And if you use cooked shrimp it will be on the table in seconds! Well, maybe not seconds...but you get the idea.

Serves 2 cal 193 carbs 15.2g protein 19.4g fat 6.4g

Heat a wok over high heat until smoking and add the canola oil. Add the garlic, ginger, and chile and stir-fry for a few seconds to release their aroma. Add the shrimp and let sear and brown for a few seconds, then flip them over and cook for 1 minute. Season with the Shaoxing rice wine or dry sherry.

Add the water chestnuts and toss well, then add the chili bean paste, honey, and light soy sauce and toss for a few seconds to mix the sauces well.

Garnish with the scallions and serve immediately.

Lobster Tails, Baby Asparagus, and Eggs in Hot Bean Sauce

1 tablespoon canola oil

2 garlic cloves, crushed and finely chopped

knob of fresh ginger, peeled and grated

1 red chile, seeded and finely chopped

7 ounces cooked fresh lobster or crayfish tails, sliced into 1-inch cubes

1 tablespoon Shaoxing rice wine or dry sherry

4 ounces baby asparagus spears, cut on an angle into 1-inch slices (about ¾ cup)

1 teaspoon yellow bean paste

½ teaspoon dark soy sauce

1 tablespoon low-sodium light soy sauce

½ cup hot vegetable stock

1 large egg, lightly beaten

1 teaspoon cornstarch blended with 1 tablespoon cold water

2 scallions, sliced into strips and soaked in iced water for 5 minutes to curl

This is a decadent stir-fry using lobster tails and the freshest baby asparagus in season. Pungent and aromatic with a hint of chili spice, it is perfect for dinner guests and fuss free to make. You can turn this into a saucy noodle dish—just up the quantities for the sauce and seasoning, add cooked thin egg noodles at the end, and wok it all together.

Serves 2 cal 238 carbs 7.8g protein 28.5g fat 10.4g

Heat a wok over high heat until smoking and add the canola oil. Add the garlic, ginger, and chile and stir-fry for a few seconds to release their aroma. Add the cooked lobster or crayfish and toss for 5 seconds. Season with the Shaoxing rice wine or dry sherry, then add the asparagus and toss for 10 seconds. Drizzle in a tablespoon of cold water around the edge of the wok to create steam to help cook the asparagus. Add the yellow bean paste, dark soy sauce, and light soy sauce and toss for 10 seconds, then add the hot vegetable stock and bring to a boil.

Stir in the beaten egg and bring back to a boil. Add the blended cornstarch and stir in to thicken the sauce and bring all the flavors together.

Garnish with the scallion curls and serve immediately.

> **CHING'S TIP**
> Work quickly to avoid overcooking the lobster.

Spicy Oyster Sauce Squid with Green Bell Peppers

1 tablespoon canola oil

1 medium white onion, halved and cut into slices

1 red chile, seeded and finely chopped

7 ounces whole baby squid

1 tablespoon Shaoxing rice wine or dry sherry

1 green bell pepper, seeded and sliced into ½-inch cubes

1 tablespoon low-sodium light soy sauce

1 teaspoon oyster sauce

½ teaspoon dark soy sauce

1 tablespoon fresh lemon juice

pinch of sugar

I love how the savory-sour combination of the oyster sauce and rice vinegar complements the delicate flavor of the baby squid. However, be careful you don't overcook the squid as it can all too quickly turn to rubber. The trick is to sear it very quickly in a very hot pan. Don't take your eye off it.

Serves 2 cal 182 carbs 11.8g protein 17.4g fat 7.6g

Heat a wok over high heat until smoking and add the canola oil. Add the onion and toss over high heat for 20 seconds until seared, softened, and brown at the edges. Add the chile and baby squid and toss for 10 seconds, then season with the Shaoxing rice wine or
dry sherry.

Add the green bell pepper and toss for 1 minute. Drizzle a tablespoon of cold water around the edge of the wok to create steam to help cook the pepper. Cook for another minute, then season with the light soy sauce, oyster sauce, dark soy sauce, lemon juice, and sugar and serve immediately.

Hot and Sour Mackerel Fillets on Spinach and Romaine

For the dressing
1 tablespoon low-sodium light soy sauce
1 tablespoon rice vinegar
pinch of dried chile flakes
pinch of sugar
1 tablespoon toasted sesame oil
1 teaspoon chili oil

For the stir-fry
7 ounces mackerel fillet, sliced into ½-inch thick strips
pinch of Chinese five-spice powder
pinch of sea salt
pinch of ground black pepper
1 tablespoon cornstarch
1 tablespoon canola oil
2 garlic cloves, crushed and finely chopped
1 red chile, seeded and finely chopped
1 tablespoon Shaoxing rice wine or dry sherry

To garnish and serve
4 to 5 romaine lettuce leaves, sliced into 1-inch pieces
4 ounces spinach leaves
1 scallion, finely sliced

To me, this dish is the perfect combination of hot and cold and light and fresh. I especially like how the crunchy romaine and fresh spinach leaves contrast with the hot-sour dressing.

Serves 2 cal 420 carbs 13.8g protein 21.7g fat 31.3g

Whisk together all the ingredients for the dressing in a bowl, then set aside.

Put the mackerel strips in a small bowl and season with the five-spice powder, sea salt, and ground black pepper, then dust with the cornstarch.

Heat a wok over high heat until smoking and add the canola oil. Add the garlic and red chile and toss for a few seconds. Add the mackerel strips and allow to sear on one side for 5 seconds, deglaze with
1 tablespoon of Shaoxing rice wine, then use a spatula to carefully lift and turn the fillets. Cook for 30 seconds over medium heat to brown the other side.

Take off the heat and place on a bed of romaine lettuce and spinach. Drizzle with the dressing, garnish with the scallion, and serve immediately.

DF

Lacassa Soup—Shrimp and Vermicelli Rice Noodle Soup

For the hot and sour fish paste
1 tablespoon Shaoxing rice wine
    or dry sherry
juice of 1 lime
1 teaspoon sambal oelek or a
    good chili sauce
1 teaspoon fermented fish paste
2 tablespoons fish sauce
1 teaspoon brown sugar

For the stir-fry
2 tablespoons canola oil
3 garlic cloves, finely chopped
1 large cayenne chile, seeded and
    finely chopped
2 medium scallions, sliced into
    3/4-inch pieces
6 ounces raw shrimp
2 dried kaffir lime leaves
2 cups good-quality hot fish
    stock
1 cup boiling water
3 1/2 ounces (3 small blocks)
    dried vermicelli rice noodles,
    presoaked in warm water for
    10 minutes, then drained
pinch of salt
pinch of ground white pepper

To serve
small handful of fresh cilantro
    sprigs
lime wedges

Typically eaten on Christmas Eve, a *lacassa* soup is thought to be a Portuguese/Macanese variation of the Malaysian laksa—a coconut-based curry soup. Traditionally, it consists of onions, *balichao* (a fermented fish paste), and shrimp, sautéed in lard. Fresh shellfish stock and vermicelli rice noodles are then added and the dish is seasoned with salt and ground white pepper. Here, I have created my own version by making a pungent spicy paste and combining it with good fish stock to make the perfect salty, fishy, spicy, sour backdrop for fresh shrimp and al dente vermicelli rice noodles.

Serves 2 cal 400 carbs 49.5g protein 23.4g fat 13.2g

Whisk together all the ingredients for the hot and sour fish paste, then set aside.

Heat a wok over high heat until smoking and add the canola oil. Add the garlic, chile, and scallions and stir-fry for a few seconds to release their aroma. Add the shrimp and stir-fry for a few seconds, then as they start to turn pink, add the hot and sour fish paste and stir quickly. Add the kaffir lime leaves and quickly pour in the hot stock together with the boiling water. Add the vermicelli rice noodles and stir for 2 minutes, then season with salt and ground white pepper.

Remove from the heat and transfer to serving bowls. Garnish with cilantro sprigs and serve immediately with lime wedges.

Clams in Shrimpy Hot Black Bean Sauce

1 tablespoon canola oil

2 garlic cloves, crushed and finely chopped

knob of fresh ginger, peeled and grated

2 red chiles, seeded and finely chopped

1 tablespoon dried shrimp, deep fried and crushed

1 tablespoon fermented salted black beans, rinsed and crushed

1¼ pounds littleneck clams (discard any where the shells remain open when tapped)

2 tablespoons Shaoxing rice wine or dry sherry

¾ cup hot vegetable stock

1 tablespoon low-sodium light soy sauce

1 tablespoon cornstarch blended with 2 tablespoons cold water

2 scallions, sliced into strips and soaked in iced water for 5 minutes to curl

I love clams cooked in a spicy Chinese black bean sauce. The saltiness of the black beans works so well with the sweetness of the clams and the dried fried baby shrimp provide a rich, pungent umami taste. You can turn this into a more substantial dish by adding cooked rice or mung bean glass noodles at the end.

Serves 2 cal 240 carbs 16.5g protein 18.8g fat 11.4g

Heat a wok over high heat until smoking and add the canola oil. Add the garlic, ginger, chiles, shrimp pieces, and fermented salted black beans and stir-fry for 10 seconds to release their aroma. Add the clams and toss for 10 seconds. As the clam shells start to open, season with the Shaoxing rice wine or dry sherry. Discard any clams that remain closed.

Add the hot vegetable stock and bring to a boil, then season with the light soy sauce and stir in the blended cornstarch to thicken the sauce.

Transfer to a serving plate, garnish with the scallion curls, and serve.

Wok-seared Miso Sea Bass with Shiitake and Bok Choy

1 tablespoon miso paste

knob of fresh ginger, peeled and grated

2 x 7-ounce sea bass fillets, skin on

2 tablespoons canola oil

2 tablespoons mirin

1 tablespoon low-sodium light soy sauce

juice of 1 lemon

For the bok choy

1 tablespoon canola oil

1 red chile, seeded and finely chopped

4 fresh shiitake mushrooms, cut into ½-inch thick slices

7 ounces bok choy leaves

1 tablespoon low-sodium light soy sauce

This is a simple but very tasty meal, perfect with jasmine rice or on its own. You can use sustainable cod from Icelandic waters, but just cook for a little longer since it is meatier.

Serves 2 cal 570 carbs 14.1g protein 43.8g fat 37g

Put the miso paste into a small bowl, add a tablespoon of cold water, and whisk well, then stir in the grated ginger. Add the sea bass fillets and turn to coat in the mixture.

Heat a wok over high heat until smoking and add 1 tablespoon canola oil. Add the chile and stir-fry for a few seconds to release its aroma. Add the fresh shiitake slices and toss for a few seconds, then add the bok choy leaves and toss for 1 minute. Season with the light soy sauce, then transfer to a serving plate and cover with foil.

Wipe out the wok and return to the heat, then add the 2 tablespoons canola oil. Add the sea bass fillets, skin side down, and press down onto the fish to prevent the fillets from curling up. Cook for 1 to 2 minutes until the skin is crisp and the fish has turned opaque, then flip the fish over to brown the other side. Season with the mirin and light soy sauce, then take off the heat and place on top of the bok choy. Drizzle with the lemon juice and serve immediately.

10 mins

5 mins

DF

Sweet and Sour Baby Squid with Chile and Kumquats

1 tablespoon canola oil

2 garlic cloves, finely chopped

knob of fresh ginger, peeled and grated

1 red chile, seeded and finely chopped

9 ounces baby squid, sliced into rings

½ teaspoon dark soy sauce

3 tablespoons mirin

2 tablespoons low-sodium light soy sauce

2 tablespoons sweet chili sauce

juice of 1 lime

For the garnish

a large handful of spinach leaves

4 fresh kumquats, finely sliced

small handful of bean sprouts

a large handful of fresh cilantro, finely chopped

This is a quick, fresh tasting dish that is perfect for summer months. Baby squid is wok-fried with Chinese aromatics, seasoned with sweet mirin, soy sauce, and sweet chili sauce, and dressed with zingy lime, kumquats, and pungent cilantro. Serve on spiralized zucchini for a low-carb meal.

Serves 2 cal 280 carbs 26.2g protein 23.1g fat 9.2g

Heat a wok over high heat until smoking and add the canola oil. Add the garlic, ginger, and chile and stir-fry for a few seconds to release their aroma. Add the squid and toss for 15 seconds, then season with a small drop of dark soy sauce and toss to coat and color the squid well. Add the mirin, light soy sauce, and sweet chili sauce and season with the lime juice.

Arrange the spinach leaves on two plates and pour the stir-fry over the top. Garnish with the kumquats, bean sprouts, and cilantro and serve immediately.

* plus 5 mins in the oven

DF

Chongqing Crispy Shrimp

For the shrimp
¾ cup potato flour
sea salt
ground white pepper
2 eggs, lightly beaten
1 cup panko bread crumbs
7 ounces jumbo shrimp, shelled,
    deveined, tail on
oil spray

For the stir-fry
1 tablespoon canola oil
1 red chile, seeded and finely
    chopped
a large handful of dried "heaven-
    facing" chiles or other
    medium-hot chile pepper
2 tablespoons Sichuan
    peppercorns
1 red bell pepper, seeded and
    sliced into 1-inch chunks
1 tablespoon Chinkiang black
    rice or balsamic vinegar
a large handful of roasted
    peanuts
a large pinch of salt
a large pinch of Chinese five-
    spice powder
dash of chili oil
dash of toasted sesame oil
2 scallions, sliced into strips,
    soaked in ice cold water
    to curl

Here I bake the battered shrimp rather than frying them, which is a lot lighter and healthier and they still turn out lovely and crispy. Please note, the Sichuan pepper and dried chiles are not for eating but to impart a wonderful numbing spicy hit to the dish. It's traditional to leave them in the dish and eat around them.

Serves 2 cal 688 carbs 89.4g protein 36.2g fat 23g

Preheat the oven to 350°F.

Start with the shrimp: Season the potato flour with salt and ground white pepper. Put the potato flour, eggs, and panko bread crumbs into three separate bowls. Dust each shrimp in the seasoned flour, then dip into the egg, and then into the bread crumbs and coat well. Set on a baking sheet. Continue until all the shrimp are done in this way. Spray the breaded shrimp generously with the oil spray. Place in the oven and cook for 5 minutes until the shrimp are cooked through and golden. Remove and set aside.

Heat a wok over high heat until smoking and add the canola oil, then add the red chile, dried chiles, and Sichuan peppercorns and stir-fry for a few seconds to release their aroma. Add the red bell pepper and toss for 10 seconds, then season with the black rice vinegar. Add the roasted peanuts and toss to combine, then add the shrimp, toss together, and season with a generous pinch of sea salt, the five-spice powder, chili oil, and toasted sesame oil. Add the scallions and toss for 30 seconds, then serve.

Steamed Haddock with Wok-fried Honey Glazed Ham and Edamame beans

2 haddock fillets, skinned
1 tablespoon Shaoxing rice wine
pinch of sea salt flakes
pinch of ground white pepper
1 tablespoon canola oil
knob of fresh ginger, peeled and grated
1 red chile, seeded and finely chopped
5 ounces honey glazed ham, diced into ¼-inch cubes (about 1 cup)
1 tablespoon Shaoxing rice wine or dry sherry
1½ cups edamame beans
¼ cup vegetable stock
1 tablespoon low-sodium light soy sauce
1 teaspoon cornstarch blended with 1 tablespoon cold water
1 teaspoon toasted sesame oil
steamed jasmine rice, to serve

This fish dish is very easy to make. You steam-cook the haddock in the wok using either a stainless steamer rack or a bamboo steamer and then keep it warm in a low oven while you prepare the delicious wok-fried sauce. The latter is inspired by fava beans with honey glazed ham, a popular dish in Hunan. If you prefer, you can substitute a small block of finely diced smoked tofu for the haddock.

Serves 2 cal 470 carbs 15.8g protein 51.7g fat 20.8g

Place the fish fillets on a heatproof plate. Season with Shaoxing rice wine, sea salt, and ground white pepper. Place the plate in a bamboo steamer or stainless steel steaming rack, and set over a wok half-filled with hot water. Cover with the lid and steam-cook the fish for 6 to 7 minutes (depending on the thickness of the fillets) until the flesh is opaque white and flakes apart when touched with a fork. Carefully remove the fish from the wok, cover with foil, and keep warm. Pour the water from the wok.

Heat the wok over high heat and add the canola oil. Add the ginger and chile and toss for 10 seconds to release their aroma. Then add the ham and cook, tossing for 10 seconds, searing the edges. Add the edamame beans and toss for 10 seconds. Add the Shaoxing rice wine and vegetable stock. Season to taste with the soy sauce, then stir in the blended cornstarch to thicken the sauce. Finally, add a dash of toasted sesame oil. Transfer the fish to a serving plate, pour the hot sauce over the fish, and serve.

20 mins*

5 mins

* includes cooking the rice

DF

1 tablespoon canola oil
knob of fresh ginger, peeled and grated
4 ounces fresh shiitake mushrooms, rinsed, dried, and cut into ¼-inch slices
2 tablespoons low-sodium light soy sauce
4 ounces haricots verts, sliced into ¼-inch rounds (about 1 cup)
1 x 8-ounce can bamboo shoots, drained and diced into 5 x ¼-inch pieces
3 tablespoons Shaoxing rice wine or dry sherry
1½ cups cooked jasmine or basmati rice (¾ cup uncooked)
⅓ cup roasted peanuts
1 large smoked mackerel fillet, flaked into 1-inch pieces
pinch of ground white pepper
1 tablespoon toasted sesame oil
small handful of goji berries, rehydrated in warm water for 4 minutes, then drained
1 tablespoon black sesame seeds

Smoked Mackerel, Shiitake Mushroom, Bamboo, and Goji Berry Rice

This dish reminds me of my grandmother's cooking. The green beans add a nice crunch, and the goji berries a pop of sweetness, plus the black sesame seeds give texture and flavor.

Serves 2 cal 721 carbs 64g protein 27.4g fat 40.6g

Heat a wok over high heat until smoking and add the canola oil. Add the ginger and stir-fry for a few seconds, then add the shiitake mushrooms and stir-fry for 15 seconds. Season with half the soy sauce and toss for 10 seconds.

Add the green beans and bamboo shoots and toss for 30 seconds, then add the Shaoxing rice wine. Once it has evaporated add the cooked rice and peanuts and toss together well. Add the smoked mackerel and toss together well.

Season to taste with more soy sauce, toasted sesame oil, and white pepper. Add the goji berries and sprinkle with black sesame seeds. Serve immediately, straight from the wok.

Chicken

DF

Fish Fragrant Chicken and Eggplant

For the chicken

7 ounces boneless chicken
    thighs, sliced into ½-inch
    strips
pinch of sea salt flakes
pinch of ground white pepper
1 teaspoon cornstarch

For the sauce

½ cup cold vegetable stock
1 tablespoon low-sodium light
    soy sauce
1 tablespoon Chinkiang black
    rice or balsamic vinegar
1 tablespoon cornstarch

For the stir-fry

2 tablespoons canola oil
7 ounces eggplant, sliced into
    batons
2 garlic cloves, crushed and
    finely chopped
1-inch piece of fresh ginger,
    peeled and grated
1 medium red chile, seeded and
    finely chopped
1 tablespoon chili bean sauce
1 tablespoon Shaoxing rice wine
    or dry sherry
1 scallion, finely sliced

This recipe is an adaptation of one of my favorite Sichuan dishes. It does not contain any fish but is called "Fish fragrant," or *Yu Siang* because it uses a good savory stock. You can add more or less to this dish and vary it with tofu, ground pork, or shiitake mushrooms and serve it with steamed jasmine rice. It's delish and packs a punch!

Serves 2 cal 365 carbs 21.1g protein 23g fat 21.7g

Place the chicken in a bowl and season with the salt, white pepper, and cornstarch.

Whisk together all the ingredients for the sauce in a bowl, then set aside. Heat a wok over high heat and as the wok starts to smoke add 1 tablespoon canola oil. Add the eggplant and stir-fry for 5 minutes until softened and brown. During this process, keep adding ¼ cup of water in small drops around the edge of the wok to create some steam to help cook and soften the eggplant.

Transfer to a plate. Reheat the wok and add another tablespoon of canola oil. Add the garlic, ginger, chile, and chili bean sauce and cook together for a few seconds. Then add the chicken strips and cook over high heat for 1 minute until they start to turn brown and opaque. Season with the Shaoxing rice wine or dry sherry and stir-fry for 3 minutes until the chicken is cooked all the way through. Return the eggplant to the wok, pour in the sauce, and simmer over medium heat for 3 minutes. Sprinkle the scallion over the top and serve immediately.

Speedy Spicy Singapore Noodles

1 tablespoon canola oil

2 garlic cloves, finely chopped

knob of fresh ginger, peeled and grated

2 red chiles, seeded and finely chopped

4 fresh shiitake mushrooms, sliced ¼-inch thick

1 cup cooked shredded chicken breast

4 ounces cooked shrimp

1 teaspoon ground turmeric

1 tablespoon Shaoxing rice wine or dry sherry

2 cups cooked vermicelli rice noodles (6 ounces uncooked)

small handful of bean sprouts

2 scallions, finely sliced on an angle

2 tablespoons low-sodium light soy sauce

1 tablespoon oyster sauce

1 large egg, lightly beaten

½ teaspoon dried red chile flakes

pinch of freshly ground white pepper

dash of toasted sesame oil

fresh cilantro leaves

This is one of the best Asian fusion dishes as the combination of dried chiles and turmeric with Chinese noodles works every time. Most supermarkets also now sell cooked vermicelli noodles in the fresh produce aisle so this dish makes an incredibly easy and speedy meal—great for a casual midweek supper or even when you're entertaining.

Serves 2 cal 576 carbs 70.3g protein 38.6g fat 16.6g

Heat a wok over high heat until smoking and add the canola oil. Add the garlic, ginger, and red chiles and cook for a few seconds, then add the mushrooms, chicken, and shrimp and toss for 20 seconds.

Add the turmeric and cook for another 10 seconds, then pour the Shaoxing rice wine or dry sherry around the edge of the wok. Add the rice noodles, bean sprouts, and scallions and toss for 20 seconds, ensuring that all the noodles are coated with the turmeric and the whole dish is uniform yellow in color. Add a small dash of water around the edge of the wok to help create some steam, then season with the light soy and oyster sauces and toss for 1 minute to combine the seasoning.

Make a well in the center of the noodles and pour in the beaten egg, then stir to combine and coat the noodles with the egg. Sprinkle with the dried chile, ground white pepper, and toasted sesame oil and give it one last stir.

Transfer to a serving plate, garnish with fresh cilantro, and serve immediately.

Chicken and Crispy Vegetables

For the chicken

3 small boneless chicken thighs, sliced into strips

1 teaspoon dark soy sauce

½ teaspoon Chinese five-spice powder

pinch of ground white pepper

1 tablespoon cornstarch

For the sauce

¼ cup cold water

1 tablespoon low-sodium light soy sauce

1 tablespoon oyster sauce

1 tablespoon rice vinegar

1 teaspoon cornstarch

For the stir-fry

1 tablespoon peanut oil

2 garlic cloves, finely chopped

knob of fresh ginger, peeled and grated

1 tablespoon Shaoxing rice wine or dry sherry

½ cup carrots, cut into julienne strips

½ cup baby corn, sliced in half

½ cup sliced water chestnuts

½ cup broccoli, cut into florets

½ cup snow peas

½ cup bean sprouts

1 scallion, cut on an angle into 1-inch slices

1 teaspoon toasted sesame oil

The secret to a good stir-fry is very simple—well-seasoned meat together with crispy, crunchy vegetables—and this dish delivers this in spades. The real star is the Chinese five-spice and the dark soy sauce as together they coat the vegetables in a rich, savory flavor that tastes like a little bit of magic. You can also use pork loin strips instead of chicken if you prefer.

Serves 2 cal 402 carbs 24.1g protein 31.4g fat 20.7g

Place the chicken strips in a bowl and season with the dark soy sauce, five-spice powder, and ground white pepper and coat to mix well. Dust with the cornstarch.

Whisk together all the ingredients for the sauce in a bowl, then set aside.

Heat a wok over high heat until smoking and add the peanut oil. Add the garlic and ginger and toss for a few seconds, then add the seasoned chicken strips. Leave for 30 seconds to sear and color, then flip the strips over, season with the Shaoxing rice wine or dry sherry, and stir-fry for 2 to 3 minutes until the chicken is cooked through and opaque.

Add all the vegetables from the carrots to the scallion and stir-fry for 2 minutes to wilt the vegetables. Give the sauce a stir, then pour onto the vegetables and cook for 30 seconds until the liquid has thickened and the vegetables are glazed but still crisp. Season with the toasted sesame oil and serve immediately.

Chicken Teriyaki with Green Bell Peppers

For the sauce

1 tablespoon sake or rice wine

2 tablespoons mirin

2 tablespoons low-sodium light soy sauce

1 teaspoon superfine sugar

For the stir-fry

1 tablespoon canola oil

2 garlic cloves, finely chopped

knob of fresh ginger, peeled and grated

9 ounces boneless chicken thighs, sliced into ½-inch x 1-inch strips

1 tablespoon sake

1 green bell pepper, seeded and sliced into ½-inch thick strips

large pinch of freshly ground black pepper

For the garnish

1 scallion, finely sliced

pinch of black sesame seeds

I love the Japanese teriyaki marinade as it's super-delicious and the perfect sauce for a fabulous stir-fry. Here, also, the green bell peppers provide the perfect fresh and crunchy accompaniment. I like using juicy chicken thighs but you can also use a chunky piece of sirloin steak and slice it into strips. Quick, easy, and delicious—you'll have dinner on the table in minutes!

Serves 2 cal 360 carbs 16.2g protein 28.1g fat 18.6g

Whisk together all the ingredients for the sauce in a small bowl, then set aside.

Heat a wok over high heat until smoking and add the canola oil, then add the garlic and ginger and stir-fry for a few seconds to release their aroma. Add the chicken and cook until seared and browned at the edges. Season with the sake and stir-fry for 2 seconds. Add the green bell pepper and stir-fry for 10 seconds, then pour in the sauce and bring to a simmer. Cook until the sauce starts to reduce and you end up with a slightly sticky shine on the chicken and peppers. Season with a large pinch of freshly ground black pepper, then transfer to a serving plate.

Garnish with the scallion and black sesame seeds and serve immediately.

5 mins

7 mins

DF

Three-cup Chicken

9 ounces boneless chicken thighs, sliced into ½-inch x 1-inch cubes
pinch of sea salt flakes
pinch of ground white pepper
1 tablespoon cornstarch
1 tablespoon canola oil
a large knob of fresh ginger, peeled and cut into large slices
2 garlic cloves, squashed but left whole
1 red chile, sliced into rings
¼ cup Shaoxing rice wine or dry sherry, plus 1 tablespoon
¼ cup low-sodium light soy sauce
¼ cup toasted sesame oil
1 teaspoon superfine sugar
8 to 10 leaves Taiwanese nine-pagoda basil or Thai sweet basil leaves

This is a classic Taiwanese recipe that is perfect for a quick and speedy supper. It's called Three-cup Chicken because traditionally it uses 1 cup of soy sauce, 1 cup of rice wine, and 1 cup of toasted sesame oil—in this recipe there's not quite 1 cup of each but certainly equal measures of all three. If Japan is famous for inventing Teriyaki sauce, Taiwan is famous for it's Three-cup Chicken sauce. The sweet basil at the end imparts an aniseed aroma and taste, which pairs perfectly with this dish. If you can't get Taiwanese basil, try Thai sweet basil or sweet basil.

Serves 2 cal 561 carbs 17.2g protein 27.8g fat 42.9g

Place the chicken in a bowl, add the salt and ground white pepper, and then dust with the cornstarch. Set aside.

Heat a wok over high heat until smoking and add the canola oil. Add the ginger slices and fry until crispy and golden, then add the garlic and red chile and toss for a few seconds to release their aroma. Add the chicken pieces and leave for 10 seconds to sear and color, then flip them over. Season with 1 tablespoon Shaoxing rice wine or dry sherry and stir-fry for 2 to 3 minutes over high heat until the chicken is almost cooked. Add the light soy sauce, the ¼ cup rice wine or dry sherry, the toasted sesame oil, and sugar and cook for 5 minutes until the liquid has almost evaporated. The chicken should have a dark brown, slightly sticky shine. Add the basil leaves and toss through to wilt, then take off the heat and serve immediately.

Spicy Lemongrass Chicken with Cashews

3 small boneless chicken thighs, sliced into ½-inch thick strips
pinch of sea salt flakes
pinch of ground white pepper
1 tablespoon cornstarch
1 tablespoon canola oil
1 onion, halved and sliced
1 garlic clove, crushed and finely chopped
knob of fresh ginger, peeled and grated
1 stalk of lemongrass, sliced into 1-inch pieces
1 tablespoon Shaoxing rice wine or dry sherry
1 green bell pepper, seeded and sliced into julienne strips
½ cup hot chicken stock
1 teaspoon brown sugar
1 tablespoon low-sodium light soy sauce
1 teaspoon fish sauce
½ teaspoon dark soy sauce
2 large scallions, cut on an angle into ½-inch slices
small handful of roasted cashews
10 Thai basil leaves

This is a tasty "fusion"-style stir-fry—I love mixing Chinese and Thai ingredients for a mash-up of Asian flavors. After all, the Dai people in Thailand minority originated from Yunnan Province in China. Here, I have taken creative license and combined Shaoxing rice wine with flavors of lemongrass, fish sauce, and Thai basil. This works wonderfully well and gives a addictive intense umami flavor to the stir-fry.

Serves 2 cal 439 carbs 25.6g protein 31.6g fat 24.7g

Place the chicken strips in a bowl, season with sea salt and ground white pepper, and dust with the cornstarch. Set aside.

Heat a wok over high heat until smoking and add the canola oil. Toss in the onion slices, garlic, ginger, and lemongrass and stir-fry for a few seconds to release their aroma. Add the chicken and cook for 10 seconds until seared and browned, then flip the meat over and stir-fry for 2 minutes. As it starts to turn opaque, season and deglaze the wok with the Shaoxing rice wine or dry sherry. Stir-fry for another 1 to 2 minutes until the chicken is completely cooked through.

Add the green bell pepper strips and toss for 30 seconds, then add the hot stock, brown sugar, light soy sauce, fish sauce, and dark soy sauce and toss in the scallions and cashews. Cook, stirring to mix well.

Just before serving, add the Thai basil leaves and toss together well.

Chicken with Chinese Curry Sauce

7 ounces boneless, skinless chicken breast, cut into 1-inch chunks

pinch of sea salt flakes

pinch of ground white pepper

1 tablespoon cornstarch

1 tablespoon peanut oil

1 garlic clove, crushed and finely chopped

knob of fresh ginger, peeled and grated

1 green chile, seeded and finely chopped

½ white onion, sliced

1 tablespoon Shaoxing rice wine or dry sherry

1 small carrot, sliced diagonally into oval pieces

handful of broccoli florets

1 scallion, finely chopped

For the curry sauce

¾ cup cold fresh chicken stock

1 star anise

1 teaspoon ground turmeric

½ teaspoon Madras hot curry powder

1 teaspoon brown sugar

1 tablespoon cornstarch

This Chinese chicken curry is similar to what you would get from a Chinese takeaway. Mildy spicy and sweet, it's a warm and comforting dish, perfect for winter and delicious with jasmine rice.

Serves 2 cal 288 carbs 28.2g protein 28.8g fat 7.6g

Put the chicken in a bowl, add the salt and white pepper, then dust with the cornstarch and set aside. Whisk together all the ingredients for the curry sauce in a bowl, then set aside.

Heat a wok over high heat until smoking and add the peanut oil, garlic, ginger, chile, and sliced onion and stir-fry for a few seconds to release their aroma. Add the chicken and let it settle for 10 seconds to sear and brown, then flip it over. Add the Shaoxing rice wine or dry sherry and toss the chicken for 2 minutes until cooked.

Add the carrot and broccoli and toss for 1 minute, then drizzle a tablespoon of cold water around the edge of the wok to create steam to help cook the vegetables. Pour in the sauce and bring to a boil.

Transfer to a serving plate, garnish with the scallion, and serve immediately.

Lemon Chicken

1 tablespoon potato flour

1 large egg, lightly beaten

1½ cups bread crumbs or Panko
bread crumbs

9 ounces boneless, skinless
chicken breast, butterflied
in half

pinch of Chinese five-spice
powder

1 teaspoon lemon zest

pinch of dried chile flakes

pinch of sea salt

pinch of ground black pepper

3½ cups canola oil

1 scallion, finely sliced

For the lemon sauce

1 teaspoon freshly grated ginger

1 tablespoon Shaoxing rice wine
or dry sherry

¾ cup hot vegetable stock

juice of 1 lemon

1 teaspoon sugar

pinch of sea salt flakes

1 teaspoon low-sodium light soy
sauce

1 tablespoon cornstarch blended
with 2 tablespoons cold water

**This is a Chinese takeaway classic and delicious served
with steamed rice or noodles. It may not be the most
straightforward stir-fry recipe, but it was too delicious to
leave out. Enjoy!**

Serves 2 cal 658 carbs 99.7g protein 44.5g fat 11.7g

Put the potato flour, beaten egg, and bread crumbs in three
separate bowls. Put the chicken breast into a large shallow bowl
and season with the five-spice powder, lemon zest, chile flakes,
salt, and ground black pepper. Turn it to coat well, then dip the
chicken first in the potato flour, then in the beaten egg, and then
in the bread crumbs to coat well.

Fill a wok to less than halfway with the canola oil. Heat the oil
to 350ºF or until a piece of bread dropped in turns golden in
15 seconds. Using a spider or slotted metal spoon, gently lower
the bread-crumbed chicken into the oil and fry for 5 minutes
until golden brown. Insert a toothpick into the chicken and make
sure it comes out clean to ensure the chicken breast is cooked
through. Drain the chicken on paper towels and keep covered
with foil.

To make the lemon sauce, pour the oil from the wok into a
heatproof bowl through a strainer. Retain 1 teaspoon of oil in the
wok and reheat the wok over high heat. Add the ginger and stir-
fry for 2 seconds, then add the Shaoxing rice wine or dry sherry.
Pour in the vegetable stock and bring to a boil. Add the lemon
juice, sugar, and sea salt, then season with the light soy sauce.
Stir in the blended cornstarch to thicken the sauce.

Slice the chicken onto serving plates and pour the lemon sauce
over, then garnish with the scallion. Serve with steamed greens.

DF

Sesame Chicken

1 tablespoon canola oil

2 garlic cloves, crushed and finely chopped

knob of fresh ginger, peeled and grated

9 ounces boneless chicken thighs, sliced into strips

1 tablespoon sake

1 tablespoon mirin

1 tablespoon low-sodium light soy sauce

1 tablespoon toasted sesame oil

pinch of sugar

2 scallions, finely sliced on a diagonal

2 tablespoons toasted black and white sesame seeds

This is a great savory, nutty stir-fry that is packed with flavor. You can add bean sprouts or blanched greens and toss together or even add thin Chinese egg noodles to turn this into a chow mein. Perfect served with steamed broccoli on the side or mixed in at the end, and steamed jasmine rice.

Serves 2 cal 424 carbs 7.3g protein 29.1g fat 30.2g

Heat a wok over high heat until smoking and add the canola oil. Add the garlic and ginger and toss for a few seconds to release their aroma. Add the chicken strips and let sear and brown for 10 seconds, then flip them over.

Add the sake and mirin and toss for a few seconds, then season with the light soy sauce, toasted sesame oil, and sugar. Toss to combine well, then add the scallions and toss again to mix.

Transfer to a plate, sprinkle with the toasted black and white sesame seeds, and serve with steamed broccoli and rice.

Oyster Sauce Chicken with Celery and Peanuts

9 ounces boneless chicken thighs, sliced into ½-inch strips
pinch of sea salt
pinch of ground white pepper
1 tablespoon cornstarch
1 tablespoon canola oil
2 garlic cloves, crushed and finely chopped
1 tablespoon Shaoxing rice wine or dry sherry
2 large celery ribs, sliced diagonally into 1-inch pieces
1 tablespoon low-sodium light soy sauce
1 tablespoon oyster sauce
pinch of dried chile flakes
small handful of roasted peanuts
1 teaspoon toasted sesame oil
steamed rice, to serve

This is a simple home-cooked dish, no explanations required— easy and delicious, it's a winner! Serve with steamed jasmine rice.

Serves 2 cal 402 carbs 14.2g protein 30.2g fat 25.6g

Put the chicken into a large bowl and season with the sea salt and ground white pepper, then dust with the cornstarch.

Heat a wok over high heat until smoking and add the canola oil, then add the garlic and toss for a few seconds to release its aroma. Add the chicken and let settle for 10 seconds to sear and brown, then flip the pieces over and stir-fry for 2 minutes. Add the Shaoxing rice wine or dry sherry, then add the celery and cook for less than 1 minute until softened but still crisp. Season with the light soy sauce, oyster sauce, and chile flakes and mix well.

Add the roasted peanuts and season with the toasted sesame oil. Stir well, then take off the heat and serve immediately.

Pineapple Chicken

9 ounces boneless chicken
thighs, sliced into ½-inch
cubes
pinch of sea salt
pinch of ground black pepper
1 tablespoon cornstarch
1 tablespoon canola oil
2 dried chiles, whole
1 tablespoon Shaoxing rice wine
or dry sherry
½ small pineapple, sliced into
½-inch cubes
½ red bell pepper, seeded and
sliced into ½-inch cubes
small handful of roasted cashews
(optional)
1 scallion, finely sliced
fresh cilantro leaves, to garnish

For the sauce
½ cup pineapple juice
1 tablespoon low-sodium light
soy sauce
1 tablespoon cornstarch
juice of 1 lime
1 teaspoon honey
¼ teaspoon Sriracha chili sauce

I love this dish because I'm a big fan of fresh, juicy sweet pineapples. This may seem like a long list of ingredients but it's so quick and easy to prepare once you have them all. If you are vegan, you can use smoked tofu instead of chicken and you could also turn this into a chow mein dish by adding cooked Chinese egg noodles at the end, if you wish.

Serves 2 cal 496 carbs 43.1g protein 30.1g fat 24.4g

Put the chicken in a bowl and season with the salt and pepper. Add the cornstarch and mix well.

Whisk together all the ingredients for the sauce in a small bowl, then set aside.

Heat a wok over high heat and when the wok starts to smoke, add the canola oil. Add the chiles and fry for a few seconds to release their aroma, then add the chicken pieces and stir-fry for 2 to 3 minutes. As the chicken starts to turn opaque, add the Shaoxing rice wine or dry sherry and cook for another 2 to 3 minutes until the chicken is cooked through.

Add the pineapple and red bell pepper pieces and cook for less than 30 seconds. Then pour in the sauce, bring to a boil, and boil until the sauce has reduced, is slightly sticky, and has a thicker consistency.

Add the cashews (if using), followed by the scallion and cook for 20 seconds. Stir together well, then transfer to a serving plate, garnish with fresh cilantro, and serve immediately.

Satay Chicken Stir-fry with Spicy Coconut Peanut Sauce

9 ounces boneless chicken thighs, sliced into ½-inch thick strips

½ teaspoon ground turmeric

½ teaspoon ground coriander

1 teaspoon ground lemongrass

pinch of salt

pinch of ground white pepper

1 tablespoon cornstarch

1 tablespoon canola oil

1 tablespoon Shaoxing rice wine or dry sherry

1 tablespoon low-sodium light soy sauce

juice of ½ lime

For the sauce

1 garlic clove, finely chopped

1 medium red chile, seeded and finely chopped

1 large shallot, finely chopped

½ teaspoon tamarind paste

½ teaspoon shrimp paste (optional)

1 teaspoon chili paste or Sriracha chili sauce

3 tablespoons crunchy peanut butter

1 tablespoon honey

¼ cup hot water

¾ cup reduced fat coconut milk

For the garnish

handful of bean sprouts

1 scallion, sliced on a diagonal

fresh cilantro leaves

lime wedges

This dish is inspired by my love of Indonesian-style satays—especially the spicy peanut sauce they serve with grilled satay. However, I'm taking some creative license here and turning it on its head into a delicious stir-fry. There's no need for sauce packages, just pantry ingredients and some fresh produce. This dish is delicious with jasmine rice or served on top of chunky Chinese egg noodles.

Serves 2 cal 563 carbs 26.7g protein 34.2g fat 36.6g

Put the chicken in a bowl and season with the turmeric, ground coriander, lemongrass, salt, and pepper, then add the cornstarch and toss to coat.

Put all the ingredients for the sauce except the hot water and coconut milk in a small food processor and blend to a fine paste. Transfer to a bowl, loosen with the hot water, and stir well to mix. Add the coconut milk and stir well.

Heat a wok over high heat until smoking and add the canola oil. Add the chicken pieces and let settle in the wok for 2 minutes until seared and browned, then flip over. As the chicken starts to brown, add the Shaoxing rice wine or dry sherry and stir-fry for 2 to 3 minutes until cooked through.

Pour in the sauce and stir together for 30 seconds to release the aroma, then bring to a boil. Season with the light soy sauce and lime juice to taste.

Transfer to a serving plate, top with the bean sprouts, scallion, cilantro leaves, and lime wedges and serve.

Hoisin Duck with Soy Pomegranate

For the duck marinade
½ teaspoon Chinese five-spice
    powder
1 teaspoon toasted sesame oil
½ teaspoon dark soy sauce
pinch of salt

For the stir-fry
10 ounces duck breast fillets,
    skinned and sliced into 1-inch
    strips ¼-inch thick
1 tablespoon cornstarch
1 tablespoon peanut oil
1 garlic clove, crushed and finely
    chopped
1 tablespoon freshly grated
    peeled ginger
1 tablespoon Shaoxing rice wine
    or dry sherry
3 cavolo nero leaves, washed,
    trimmed, and cut into ½-inch
    slices

For the soy pomegranate sauce
½ cup cold vegetable stock
2 tablespoons hoisin sauce
1 teaspoon honey
1 tablespoon low-sodium light
    soy sauce
¼ cup pomegranate juice
1 tablespoon cornstarch

For the garnish
⅓ cup fresh pomegranate seeds
1 scallion, trimmed and sliced on
    a diagonal

This is a delicious stir-fry using duck breast fillets. I usually like to serve it for a Chinese-style feast post-Christmas on Boxing Day. It's fuss free and the five-spice duck together with the pomegranate bring a spicy, fruity note that continues the celebrations. There may seem like a long list of ingredients, but I promise it's dead easy.

Serves 2 cal 439 carbs 38g protein 32.8g fat 18.2g

Whisk together all the ingredients for the marinade in a bowl, then add the duck and turn to coat. Let marinate for 10 minutes. Dust with the cornstarch.

Whisk together all the ingredients for the soy pomegranate sauce in another bowl, then set aside.

Heat a wok over high heat until smoking and add the peanut oil. Add the garlic and ginger and stir-fry for a few seconds to release their aroma. Add the duck and let it settle for 10 seconds to sear and brown on one side, then flip it over. Season with the Shaoxing rice wine or dry sherry. Add the cavolo nero and toss for 10 seconds until it starts to wilt, then drizzle in 1 tablespoon cold water around the edge of the wok to create some steam to help cook the kale. Toss and cook all together.

Give the soy pomegranate sauce a stir and pour into the wok, then bring to a boil gently, stirring. The sauce should thicken and become glossy.

Remove from the heat and transfer to a serving plate, garnish with the pomegranate seeds and scallion, and serve immediately with jasmine rice.

DF

Sichuan Chicken with Baby Zucchini

For the Sichuan spicy sauce

¼ cup cold water

1 teaspoon chili bean paste

1 tablespoon Chinkiang black rice or balsamic vinegar

1 tablespoon low-sodium light soy sauce

½ teaspoon brown sugar

1 teaspoon cornstarch

1 teaspoon toasted sesame oil

For the chicken

2 boneless chicken thighs, sliced thinly on an angle

pinch of cracked sea salt

pinch of ground white pepper

1 tablespoon cornstarch

For the stir-fry

1 tablespoon canola oil

2 small garlic cloves, smashed and coarsely chopped

1-inch piece of fresh ginger, peeled and finely grated

1 large red cayenne chile, seeded and sliced

1 tablespoon Shaoxing rice wine or dry sherry

7 ounces baby zucchini, cut on an angle into ¼-inch slices (about 1½ cups)

1 to 2 tablespoons cold water

This is a spicy, saucy dish that is incredibly addictive and one of my favorite dishes to cook at home. You can up the game with more vegetables if you wish and add carrots or assorted bell peppers. Serve with steamed jasmine rice.

Serves 2 cal 300 carbs 19.9g protein 20.5g fat 15.9g

Whisk together all the ingredients for the Sichuan spicy sauce in a bowl, then set aside.

In another bowl, season the chicken strips with salt and ground white pepper and then dust with the cornstarch.

Heat a wok over high heat until smoking and add the canola oil. Add the garlic, ginger, and red chile and toss for a few seconds to release their aroma. Add the chicken strips and stir-fry for 2 minutes, then as they start to turn brown, add the Shaoxing rice wine or dry sherry. Stir-fry over high heat for another 2 minutes until the chicken is tender and cooked through.

Add the zucchini slices and toss for 1 minute. Drizzle in a little cold water around the edge of the wok to create some steam to help cook the zucchini. Pour in the sauce and stir-fry for 1 minute until the zucchini has softened and the sauce has thickened. Give the mixture a final stir, then take off the heat and serve immediately with steamed rice.

DF

Hot Sweet and Sour Chicken

For the sauce

¼ cup mirin

1 teaspoon chili bean paste

2 tablespoons low-sodium light
    soy sauce

2 tablespoons rice vinegar

2 tablespoons honey

For the stir-fry

1 tablespoon canola oil

1 garlic clove, finely chopped

1-inch piece fresh ginger, peeled
    and sliced into matchsticks

2 medium red chiles, seeded and
    sliced

9 ounces boneless chicken
    thighs, sliced into ½-inch x
    1-inch strips

1 tablespoon Shaoxing rice wine
    or dry sherry

2 cups spiralized zucchini

toasted sesame seeds

This is a sweet, spicy, salty, sour dish—all my favorite flavors in one. Perfect for a quick midweek supper. You can toss the spiralized zucchini in to heat through if you prefer, or serve them raw. You can also serve this with steamed greens and jasmine rice. Whichever way you go...enjoy!

Serves 2 cal 432 carbs 34g protein 30.1g fat 19.7g

Whisk together all the ingredients for the sauce in a bowl, then set aside.

Heat a wok over high heat until smoking and add the canola oil. Add the garlic, ginger, and chiles and toss for a few seconds to release their aroma. Add the chicken and let it settle for 15 seconds to sear and brown, then flip it over and cook for 1 minute. As it starts to brown, add the Shaoxing rice wine or dry sherry and cook for another 2 minutes until the chicken is cooked through.

Pour in the sauce and stir-fry over high heat until the sauce has reduced and is glossy and thick.

Divide the spiralized zucchini between two plates, pour the hot and sour chicken over the top, sprinkle on the toasted sesame seeds for a nutty garnish, and serve immediately.

Pork, beef

& lamb

Cantonese-style Sweet and Sour Pork

9-ounce pork tenderloin, cut into
¼-inch slices
pinch of sea salt flakes
pinch of ground white pepper
1 large egg, lightly beaten
1 tablespoon cornstarch
1¾ cups peanut oil
1 knob fresh ginger, peeled and
grated
2 long dried chiles
1 red bell pepper, seeded and
cut into 1-inch chunks
1 green bell pepper, seeded and
cut into 1-inch chunks
1 x 8-ounce can of pineapple
chunks
1 tablespoon low-sodium light
soy sauce
1 tablespoon rice vinegar or cider
vinegar
½ teaspoon brown sugar
1 teaspoon cornstarch blended
with 1 tablespoon cold water

To garnish
fresh cilantro leaves
1 scallion, sliced into julienne
strips and soaked in iced
water to curl

This is a hugely popular and well recognized dish in Chinese restaurants and my favorite way to cook Cantonese-style Sweet and Sour Pork. The recipe is taken from my book *Chinese Food in Minutes*. Serve with steamed jasmine rice.

Serves 2 cal 463 carbs 35.2g protein 33.8g fat 22g

Place the pork tenderloin in a bowl and season with the salt and ground white pepper. Mix the egg and cornstarch together to create a batter. Add the pork pieces to it and coat well.

Heat a wok over high heat until smoking and fill it with the peanut oil. Heat until the oil glistens and a small piece of bread dropped in turns golden brown in 15 seconds and floats to the surface. Using a spider or slotted metal spoon, carefully add the pork slices to the oil and fry for 3 to 4 minutes until golden brown. Using chopsticks or the spider, lift out the meat and place on a plate lined with paper towels to drain any excess oil.

Pour the oil from the wok into a heatproof bowl through a strainer and save to use later. Retain 1 tablespoon of oil in the wok and heat until smoking. Add the grated ginger, dried chiles, and the bell peppers and quickly stir-fry to stop the ginger from sticking. Stir for 2 minutes, then add the pineapple chunks and their juice and bring to a simmer. Season with the light soy sauce, vinegar, and brown sugar. Then, as the liquid in the wok reduces and boils, stir in the blended cornstarch and cook until the mixture thickens. Return the pork to the wok, stir, and toss together well so the pork is covered in the sauce. Serve immediately.

1 hour*

5 mins

*includes initial cooking
of pork

DF

Twice-cooked Pork

7 ounces fatty pork belly, skin on
2 tablespoons canola oil
1 tablespoon Shaoxing rice wine
   or dry sherry
1 teaspoon chili bean paste
1 teaspoon yellow bean sauce
1 teaspoon fermented salted
   black beans, rinsed and
   crushed
2 scallions or baby leeks, sliced
   diagonally
1 teaspoon dark soy sauce
1 tablespoon low-sodium light
   soy sauce
pinch of superfine sugar
pinch of salt
pinch of freshly ground white
   pepper
1½ cups steamed jasmine rice,
   to serve

For the pickled cucumber
1 garlic clove, minced with a
   pinch of sugar
1 tablespoon rice vinegar or cider
   vinegar
1 teaspoon chili bean paste
1 teaspoon chili oil
1 tablespoon toasted sesame oil
2 small cucumbers, sliced in half
   lengthwise, seeded, then cut
   into ½-inch strips
1 fresh red cayenne chile, seeded
   and cut into small strips

If the Chinese did fried bacon, this would be it. After the pork belly slices are poached they are placed in the fridge to firm up and then sliced thinly and wok-fried with chili bean paste, yellow bean paste, and soy. The important thing is to slice the meat as finely as you can and then to fry the pork pieces so they are crisp and golden at the edges. Serve with a side of quick pickled cucumbers and plain rice. For a vegan version, use slices of smoked tofu. Truly versatile and delicious.

Serves 2 cal 692 carbs 56.7g protein 27.3g fat 41g

For the pork, pour 3 cups cold water into a large pan, add the pork, bring to a boil, and then boil for 30 minutes. Drain and let cool. When cold, transfer the meat to the fridge for 1 hour to firm up. Meanwhile, for the pickled cucumber, combine the garlic, sugar, vinegar, chili bean paste, chili oil, and sesame oil in a bowl. Add the cucumber strips and let marinate in the fridge for 20 minutes.

Remove the cucumbers from the fridge and add the fresh chile. Remove the pork from the fridge and cut into ¼-inch thick slices.

Heat a wok over high heat until smoking and add the canola oil, then the pork (or tofu). As the pork starts to brown, add the Shaoxing rice wine or dry sherry and cook until the pork has browned and the skin is slightly crisp. Add the chili bean paste, yellow bean sauce, and fermented black beans and stir-fry for 1 minute. Add the scallions or leeks and stir-fry for less than 1 minute until well mixed. Stir in both soy sauces and the sugar, then season with salt and ground white pepper.

To serve, place a spoonful of rice onto each plate and spoon the pork (or tofu) over the top, then add the pickled cucumber alongside it. Serve with more jasmine rice on the side.

10 mins

7–8 mins

DF

Zhajiang Noodles

For the noodles

1 tablespoon sesame oil

1 teaspoon dried chili sauce laced with chili oil

7 ounces wheat or Chinese egg noodles, cooked, drained, and tossed with 1 teaspoon toasted sesame oil

For the stir-fry

2 tablespoons canola oil

1 tablespoon finely chopped garlic

1 tablespoon finely chopped fresh ginger

2 tablespoons diced baby leeks

1 teaspoon Sichuan peppercorns

7 ounces smoked bacon, finely diced

1 tablespoon Shaoxing rice wine or dry sherry

1 tablespoon fragrant oil (ginger and scallion-infused oil, see Tip)

1 teaspoon dark soy sauce

¾ cup hot chicken or pork stock

1 tablespoon tian mian jiang or hoisin sauce

1 tablespoon yellow bean paste or miso

For the garnish

2 small red radishes, julienned

½ cucumber, seeded and julienned

1 scallion, finely chopped

"Zhajiang mein" means "mixed sauce noodle" and is a classic Beijing dish that is made with fresh hand-pulled noodles. There are many different variations, and some are saucier than others, but I prefer the traditional Zhajiang noodle, which is slightly drier. I also like to add minced garlic as well as the customary leeks, ginger, Shaoxing rice wine, Sichuan peppercorns, and chili oil. Here, I have used smoked bacon instead of traditional belly pork (known as the "five layers of heaven," a reference to the skin, fat, meat, fat, skin) because of their smoky salty cured flavor. The trick is to dry-fry them in the wok until the fat is slightly crispy.

Serves 2 cal 697 carbs 39.3g protein 25.3g fat 49.7g

Start with the noodles. Divide the sesame oil and chili sauce between two serving bowls. Place the cooked noodles in the bowls and set aside.

Heat a wok over high heat until smoking and add the canola oil. Add the garlic, ginger, leeks, and Sichuan peppercorns and toss in the heat for a few seconds. Then add the bacon and stir-fry for 1 minute. Add the Shaoxing rice wine or dry sherry, the fragrant oil, and dark soy sauce and stir-fry for 1 minute. Add the stock, tian mian jiang or hoisin sauce, and the yellow bean paste or miso and toss together well. Cook for 2 minutes, stirring until the pork is cooked.

Divide the pork mixture between the two bowls of noodles and garnish with the radish and cucumber matchsticks. Sprinkle with the scallion and serve immediately. To eat, toss and mix all the ingredients well.

CHING'S TIP

Heat 5 tablespoons of peanut oil. Add a pinch of salt, 1 tablespoon grated ginger and 1 tablespoon finely chopped scallion, cook for 1 minute then strain the oil into a glass jar. Keep for 5 days in a cool place.

20 mins*

5 mins

* includes cooking
the rice

DF

My Posh Yangzhou Fried Rice

2 tablespoons canola oil

3 large eggs, lightly beaten

4 fresh shiitake mushrooms, finely diced

2 ounces cooked fresh baby shrimp

2 ounces cooked honey glazed ham or Chinese roast pork, diced (about ½ cup)

1½ cups cooked jasmine rice (¾ cup uncooked)

4 ounces fresh white crabmeat

1 tablespoon low-sodium light soy sauce

1 tablespoon toasted sesame oil

pinch of sea salt

pinch of ground white pepper

1 scallion, finely sliced

chili sauce, to serve (optional)

This is a beautiful rich fried-rice dish that is perfect for entertaining. However, you can dress it up or down and even use leftovers, if you like. It was invented by Yang Shu, a Sui dynasty government official in the late sixth century, and traditionally the egg is added with the rice and coats each grain. However, I love my eggs scrambled so that golden pieces sit next to smoked Chinese ham, shiitake mushrooms, shrimp and crabmeat. It seems "posh"-er that way!

Serves 2 cal 576 carbs 49.6g protein 33.9g fat 28.2g

Heat a wok over high heat until smoking, then add 1 tablespoon canola oil. Pour in the beaten eggs and let settle for 1 to 2 minutes, then swirl the egg around the wok and, using a wooden spoon, stir to lightly scramble it. Transfer to a plate and set aside.

Reheat the wok and add the remaining canola oil. Add the mushrooms, baby shrimp, and honey glazed ham or Chinese roast pork and toss for 30 seconds. Add the rice and mix well until the rice has broken down.

Return the scrambled eggs to the wok, add the crabmeat, and season with the light soy sauce, sesame oil, salt, and white pepper to taste. Toss well to ensure the seasoning has coated all the rice grains evenly.

Garnish with sliced scallion and serve immediately with some chili sauce on the side (if you like).

Spicy Chinese Sausage, Egg and Chinese Chives

1 tablespoon canola oil

pinch of sea salt

1 garlic clove, finely chopped

2 ounces cooked Chinese sausage or chorizo, finely chopped

small handful of dried Chinese shrimp, soaked in warm water for 20 minutes, drained, and coarsely chopped

1 tablespoon Shaoxing rice wine or dry sherry

1 teaspoon pickled chiles, finely chopped, or chili sauce

bunch of Chinese chives or scallions, sliced into 2-inch pieces

3 large eggs, lightly beaten

1 tablespoon low-sodium light soy sauce

1 teaspoon toasted sesame oil

This is a traditional recipe that my grandmother used to make for me with dried Taiwanese sausages, made from 50 percent pork meat and 50 percent pork belly fat, salt, and sugar and then wind-dried. The closest alternative you can get to these are dried Cantonese-style *lap chong* sausages, which need to be pre-cooked by boiling them in water for 15 minutes. However, if you can't get them, use chorizo or smoked bacon lardons, for a spicy, salty fusion stir-fry. Either way, it will taste delicious.

Serves 2 cal 345 carbs 2.5g protein 30.4g fat 23.8g

Heat a wok over high heat until smoking and add the canola oil. Add the sea salt and let it dissolves in the hot oil. Add the garlic and chopped Chinese sausage or chorizo, followed by the dried shrimp pieces and stir-fry for 1 minute until slightly crisp. Season with the Shaoxing rice wine or dry sherry, then add the pickled chiles or chili sauce and the Chinese chives or scallions and toss for 1 minute until the chives start to wilt.

Make a small space in the middle of the wok and add the beaten eggs, then stir to scramble them. Season with the light soy sauce and toasted sesame oil and toss together.

Transfer to a serving plate and serve immediately.

DF

Ground Pork with String Beans and Soy Sauce

1 tablespoon canola oil

2 garlic cloves, crushed and finely chopped

1 red chile, seeded and finely chopped

10 ounces lean ground pork

½ teaspoon Chinese five-spice powder

1 teaspoon dark soy sauce

1 tablespoon Shaoxing rice wine or dry sherry

7 ounces string beans or haricots verts, cut on an angle into 1-inch slices (about 2 cups)

¼ cup cold vegetable stock

1 tablespoon low-sodium light soy sauce

1 teaspoon cornstarch blended with 1 tablespoon cold water

pinch of ground black pepper

1 teaspoon toasted sesame oil

I first tasted this dish in Beijing, where Pork and String Beans is a very popular example of home-style cooking. It was cooked for me by a lady who lived down a traditional Beijing *hutong* (a narrow alley) and she used slivers of pork and no cornflour so the dish was quite oily but very delicious. This is my take on it and I hope you give it a try. Perfect served with jasmine rice or you can toss in cooked noodles or your choice.

Serves 2 cal 298 carbs 8.8g protein 35.8g fat 13.7g

Heat a wok over high heat until smoking and add the canola oil. Add the garlic and chile and toss for a few seconds to release their aroma. Add the pork and let it settle in the wok for 30 seconds to brown and sear, then stir-fry for 1 minute. Add the five-spice powder and season with the dark soy sauce. Toss until the pork turns a rich brown color, then season and deglaze the wok with the Shaoxing rice wine or dry sherry.

Add the beans and toss for 2 minutes. Add the vegetable stock and bring to a boil, then season with the light soy sauce and stir in the blended cornstarch to give the dish a shine and gloss. Add a pinch of ground black pepper and season with the toasted sesame oil.

Take off the heat and serve immediately.

Scallion Potatoes with Pork

pinch of sea salt

10 ounces potatoes (about
   1 large), peeled and cut into
   thin matchsticks

2 tablespoon of canola oil

1 tablespoon finely chopped
   garlic

knob of fresh ginger, peeled and
   grated

1 red chile, seeded and finely
   chopped

9 ounces lean ground pork

1 tablespoon Shaoxing rice wine
   or dry sherry

½ teaspoon dark soy sauce

1 tablespoon oyster sauce

1 tablespoon low-sodium light
   soy sauce

3 scallions, finely chopped

1 teaspoon toasted sesame oil

a large pinch of ground black
   pepper

1 teaspoon chili oil

This comforting dish is my take on pork hash. You could easily turn it into a delicious brunch by adding a few fried or poached eggs. Great for any weekend—and especially for a hangover!

Serves 2 cal 429 carbs 34g protein 31.7g fat 19.4g

Pour 2½ cups cold water into a bowl, add the sea salt, then soak the potatoes in the salted water for 5 minutes. Drain and set aside.

Heat a wok over high heat until smoking and add the canola oil. Add the garlic, ginger, and red chile and stir-fry for a few seconds to release their aroma. Add the potatoes and cook for 2 minutes until golden and crisp. Push the ingredients in the wok to one side, heat up the center of the wok over high heat, and add another tablespoon of canola oil. Add the ground pork and let it settle for 30 seconds to crisp up and sear and brown. Once the pork starts to turn brown, add the Shaoxing rice wine or dry sherry followed by the dark soy sauce, then toss all the ingredients for another 30 seconds. Add the oyster sauce and light soy sauce and toss well together.

Add the scallions, stir to combine well, then stir-fry until the scallions have softened but still have a bite. Season with the toasted sesame oil, ground black pepper, and chili oil. Stir again, then transfer to a serving plate.

10 mins

7 mins

DF

Ginger Pork and Chinese Broccoli

For the pork

1 x 10-ounce pork loin, sliced into 1-inch flat strips

pinch of sea salt

pinch of ground white pepper

1 tablespoon cornstarch

For the stir-fry

1 tablespoon canola oil

knob of fresh ginger, peeled and sliced into matchsticks

1 tablespoon Shaoxing rice wine or dry sherry

7 ounces Chinese broccoli (gai lan), or broccolini, cut on an angle into 1-inch slices (about 2 cups)

1 teaspoon chili bean paste

2 tablespoons low-sodium light soy sauce

1 teaspoon rice vinegar

1 teaspoon toasted sesame oil

If you can find a Chinese/Asian grocer near you that stocks fresh "gai lan" (also known as Chinese broccoli), it will make this dish dreamy. The sweet crunchy stems of the broccoli pair so well with the spicy-gingery-oyster-soy flavors of this dish. If you can't find Chinese gai lan, use broccolini—it won't be the same but it will still be delicious. Perfect served with rice or cooked noodles.

Serves 2   cal 474   carbs 15.3g   protein 44.6g   fat 26.3g

Combine all the ingredients for the pork in a bowl, then set aside.

Heat a wok over high heat until smoking and add the canola oil. Add the ginger and toss for 5 seconds, then add the pork pieces and let settle in the wok for 10 seconds to brown and sear. Flip the pork over and cook for 30 seconds. Season with the Shaoxing rice wine or dry sherry and toss until all the pork is cooked through.

Add the broccoli and toss for 1 minute over high heat. Drizzle in 1 tablespoon cold water around the edges of the wok to create some steam to help cook the broccoli. Season with the chili bean paste, light soy sauce, vinegar, and toasted sesame oil and toss to mix well. Transfer to a serving plate and serve immediately.

10 mins

6 mins

DF

Cheat Char Siu Pork with Pak Choy

For the pork

9 ounces pork tenderloin, cut
   into ¼-inch slices
½ teaspoon dark soy sauce
1 teaspoon hoisin
1 teaspoon honey
pinch of sea salt flakes
pinch of ground white pepper
1 tablespoon cornstarch

For the sauce

¼ cup cold water
1 tablespoon low-sodium light
   soy sauce
1 teaspoon hoisin sauce
½ teaspoon yellow bean paste
   or miso paste

For the stir-fry

1 tablespoon canola oil
2 garlic cloves, crushed and
   finely chopped
knob of fresh ginger, peeled and
   grated
1 tablespoon Shaoxing rice wine
   or dry sherry
7 ounces bok choy leaves, sliced
   in half on a diagonal

I love the flavor of char siu pork but it takes some time to roast and if you want dinner in minutes then this is my cheat char siu pork stir-fry. Serve with steamed jasmine rice.

Serves 2 cal 323 carbs 19g protein 30.1g fat 14.2g

Put all the ingredients for the pork except the cornstarch into a bowl and turn to coat the pork. Dust with the cornstarch and set aside.

Whisk together all the ingredients for the sauce in a bowl, then set aside.

Heat a wok over high heat until smoking and add the canola oil. Add the garlic and ginger and stir-fry for a few seconds to release their aroma. Add the pork tenderloin and let it settle for 10 seconds to sear and brown, then flip it over. Add the Shaoxing rice wine or dry sherry and toss for another 5 seconds. Add the bok choy leaves, then drizzle in 1 tablespoon cold water around the edge of the wok to create some steam to help cook the bok choy. Toss for 30 seconds to wilt the leaves, then pour in the sauce and toss well.

Transfer to a serving plate and serve immediately.

* includes marinating
the pork

DF

Salty Fried Yellow Bean Pork with Baby Corn and Sugar Snap Peas

For the marinade

2 garlic cloves, crushed and
finely chopped

knob of fresh ginger, peeled
and grated

1 teaspoon yellow bean paste or
miso paste

pinch of ground black pepper

For the stir-fry

9 ounces pork loin, sliced against
the grain into ½-inch x 1-inch
strips

1 teaspoon cornstarch

1 tablespoon canola oil

1 tablespoon Shaoxing rice wine
or dry sherry

1 cup baby corn, sliced in half
diagonally

2 cups sugar snap peas

1 tablespoon low-sodium light
soy sauce

A delicious savory, porky stir-fry with crisp, crunchy vegetables. The black pepper complements the salty yellow bean paste. Perfect with jasmine rice.

Serves 2 cal 388 carbs 11.3g protein 38g fat 21.1g

Whisk together all the ingredients for the marinade in a bowl, add the pork, and let marinate for 10 minutes. Dust with the cornstarch.

Heat a wok over high heat until smoking and add the canola oil. Add the pork and let it settle for 10 seconds to sear and brown, then flip it over and stir-fry for 1 minute. Season with the Shaoxing rice wine or dry sherry, then add the baby corn and sugar snap peas and toss for 1 minute, adding a dash of water around the edge of the wok to create some steam to help cook the vegetables.

Season with the light soy sauce and serve.

Beef and Kimchi Water Chestnuts

1 x 12-ounce sirloin steak, fat trimmed off, sliced against the grain into ½-inch thick strips
pinch of sea salt flakes
pinch of ground black pepper
1 tablespoon cornstarch
1 tablespoon canola oil
knob of fresh ginger, grated
7 ounces store-bought kimchi, drained, (reserve 1 tablespoon of liquid)
½ cup water chestnuts, sliced into round coins
1 to 2 tablespoons low-sodium light soy sauce
1 teaspoon rice vinegar or cider vinegar
1 teaspoon chili oil
2 scallions, sliced on an angle, to garnish

This is a marriage made in wok heaven. The combination of delicious savory beef slices paired with the punchy Korean fermented cabbage, kimchi, is out of this world. Traditionally, it's frowned upon to stir-fry kimchi, but I think it's worth going against the rules for this one. The pungent, spicy kimchi complements the meaty beef so well; a simple but elegant dish, perfect for foodie friends.

Serves 2 cal 378 carbs 16.7g protein 43.2g fat 15.3g

Put the beef strips in a bowl, season with salt and ground black pepper, and dust with the cornstarch.

Heat a wok over a high heat and add the canola oil. Add the ginger and toss for a few seconds, then add the beef strips. Sear them on one side until brown, then turn the strips and stir-fry for 1 minute.

Add the kimchi and water chestnuts and toss together, then season with light soy sauce to taste, the vinegar, chili oil, and reserved liquid from the kimchi. Toss once more gently together, then garnish with the scallions and serve.

15 mins

5 mins

DF

Thai-style Orange Beef

For the beef
½ teaspoon Chinese five-spice
    powder
2 x 7-ounce sirloin steaks, fat
    trimmed off, sliced into ½-inch
    thick strips
pinch of sea salt
pinch of ground black pepper
1 tablespoon cornstarch

For the sauce
1 tablespoon low-sodium light
    soy sauce
1 tablespoon fish sauce
1 teaspoon superfine sugar
juice of 1 large orange
juice of 1 lime
1 tablespoon cornstarch

For the stir-fry
1 tablespoon canola oil
1 large red onion, finely sliced
    into wedges
1 stalk of lemongrass, finely
    grated
1 red chile, seeded and sliced
pinch of ground black pepper

For the garnish
2 scallions, finely sliced
small handful of fresh mint
    leaves
small handful of fresh cilantro
    leaves
watercress leaves, to serve
Sriracha chili sauce (optional)

I love the sweet, spicy, pungent flavors of Thai cuisine and this
dish is inspired by the beautiful freshness of a Thai Beef Salad
and the delicious sticky sweetness of Chinese Orange Beef.
They work perfectly together. Add cooked wide rice noodles
at the end, if you like, and toss through some cashews for a
protein-rich crunch.

Serves 2 cal 476 carbs 36.4g protein 51g fat 15.1g

Place all the ingredients for the beef in a bowl and toss together.
Set aside.

Whisk together all the ingredients for the sauce in a bowl, and
stir well to dissolve the sugar.

Heat a wok over high heat until smoking and add the canola
oil, then add the red onion and stir-fry for 10 seconds until it
starts to soften. Add the grated lemongrass and red chile and
toss for a few seconds, then add the beef and sear and brown
for 10 seconds. Flip the beef over and toss with the rest of the
ingredients for 20 seconds until the beef is colored and seared
on the outside but is still medium on the inside (cook for another
minute if you want it well-done).

Pour in the sauce and toss for 30 seconds until the flavors have
coated the beef well. Season with ground black pepper.

Take off the heat immediately and transfer to a serving plate.
Garnish with the scallions, fresh herbs, and watercress and toss
at the table before eating. For more spice, serve with a side of
your favorite chili sauce (if you like).

Sizzling Sichuan Water-cooked Beef

9 ounces beef tenderloin, fat trimmed off, cut into wafer-thin 2-inch squares (see Tip page 194)

pinch of sea salt

pinch of ground white pepper

1 tablespoon cornstarch

1 tablespoon canola oil

2 garlic cloves, crushed and finely chopped

knob of fresh ginger, peeled and grated

1 red chile, seeded and finely chopped

4 whole dried red chiles

1½ cups fresh bean sprouts

1 tablespoon Shaoxing rice wine or dry sherry

1 tablespoon chili oil

¼ cup vegetable oil

3 scallions, cut on an angle into 1-inch slices

1 to 2 tablespoons toasted whole Sichuan peppercorns

For the sauce

¾ cup cold chicken stock

1 tablespoon chili bean paste

1 tablespoon low-sodium light soy sauce

1 teaspoon toasted sesame oil

1 tablespoon cornstarch

This is my take on the Sichuan classic "Shui Tzeng Niu Rou"—Water-cooked Beef. There are many variations but I first learnt this dish from a wok master at The New World Restaurant while filming a Chinese New Year segment in London's Chinatown. Although it was a dim sum restaurant, they served other classic Chinese dishes such as this. I didn't get to take the recipe down but I couldn't forget it—it was mesmerising to watch the wok dance that took place. If you are afraid of heat, you can tone down the use of Sichuan peppercorns, but they do impart a delicious numbing heat that is highly addictive.

Serves 2 cal 634 carbs 26.2g protein 32.9g fat 46.1g

Season the beef with salt and ground white pepper and dust with the cornstarch. Whisk together all the ingredients for the sauce in a bowl, then set aside.

Heat a wok over high heat until smoking and add the canola oil, then add the garlic, ginger, red chile, and dried chiles and stir-fry for a few seconds to release their aroma. Add the bean sprouts and toss for 5 seconds, then season with the Shaoxing rice wine or dry sherry and the chili oil.

Pour in the sauce and combine well, then bring to a boil and transfer to a heatproof serving dish.

Wipe out the wok, then place back on the heat, add the vegetable oil, and heat to 350ºF using a thermometer or until a piece of bread dropped in turns golden brown in 15 seconds. Take off the heat.

Place the scallions and raw beef slices in the serving dish on top of the bean sprouts and sprinkle with the Sichuan peppercorns. Pour the sizzling hot oil over the top to cook the beef and fry the peppercorns and scallions. Serve immediately.

20* mins

6 mins

* includes cooking the rice

DF

Beef and Spinach Fried Rice

For the beef

4 ounces beef sirloin, fat trimmed off, sliced into thin strips

knob of fresh ginger, peeled and grated

pinch of sea salt flakes

pinch of ground white pepper

1 tablespoon Shaoxing rice wine or dry sherry

For the fried rice

2 tablespoons canola oil

1 garlic clove, crushed and finely chopped

7 ounces spinach leaves

1½ cups cooked basmati rice (¾ cup uncooked)

1 tablespoon low-sodium light soy sauce

1 teaspoon oyster sauce

1 tablespoon toasted sesame oil

pinch of ground white pepper

If you have some cooked basmati rice to hand, this dish is incredibly quick to make. If you want to make it carb-free then omit the rice and add some add some broccolini or Chinese cabbage to make the dish go further.

Serves 2 cal 429 carbs 43.7g protein 19.4g fat 20.7g

Combine all the ingredients for the beef in a bowl, then set aside.

Heat a wok over high heat until smoking and add 1 tablespoon canola oil. Add the garlic and stir-fry for a few seconds to release its aroma, then add the spinach and cook for 5 seconds. Add in the cooked rice and toss with the spinach for 30 seconds.

Push the rice to one side, then heat up the center of the wok and pour in the remaining canola oil. Add the beef and let it brown and sear for 10 seconds, then flip it over. Stir-fry until all the beef has coated the rice, then season with the light soy sauce, oyster sauce, and toasted sesame oil. Sprinkle with some ground white pepper and serve immediately.

> CHING'S TIP
> Work quickly so the spinach doesn't become mush.

Spicy Ponzu Beef

For the dressing
1 tablespoon low-sodium
    light soy sauce
juice of 1 lemon
pinch of superfine sugar

For the stir-fry
1 tablespoon canola oil
2 garlic cloves, crushed and
    finely chopped
1 red chile, sliced into rings
10 ounces beef sirloin, fat
    trimmed off, cut into ½-inch
    thick slices
1 tablespoon mirin
7 ounces mixed leaves (romaine,
    spinach, watercress, arugula)

For the garnish
bonito flakes
scallion, finely sliced

I love super easy and tasty, I love light stir-fried dishes like this, which can be served with a plate of vibrant greens for a delicious supper. If you can get hold of bonito (wood-smoked tuna flakes) from Japanese or Chinese supermarkets) it will impart a smoky sweet flavor to the beef.

Serves 2 cal 295 carbs 7.8g protein 37.1g fat 12.8g

Whisk together all the ingredients for the dressing in a jar, then set aside.

To prepare the beef, Heat a wok over high heat until smoking and add the canola oil. Add the garlic and chile and toss for a few seconds to release their aroma. Add the beef slices and leave for 10 seconds to sear and brown, then flip them over. Toss for 15 seconds until medium (for well-done toss for 1 minute). Season with the mirin.

Divide the salad leaves between two plates. Spoon the beef out on top of the leaves, drizzle with the dressing, garnish with the bonito flakes and scallion, and then serve.

Chili-Peanut Lamb

For the sauce

1 teaspoon chili bean paste

1 tablespoon crunchy peanut
  butter

1 tablespoon low-sodium
  light soy sauce

1 tablespoon Chinkiang black
  rice vinegar or balsamic
  vinegar

¼ cup cold water

1 teaspoon cornstarch

For the stir-fry

1 tablespoon canola oil

4 whole dried chiles

½ teaspoon ground dry-toasted
  Sichuan peppercorns

9 ounces lamb loin, sliced into
  thin strips

1 tablespoon Shaoxing rice
  wine or dry sherry

toasted sesame oil

dash of chili oil

handful of dry roasted peanuts

small handful of fresh cilantro
  leaves, finely chopped
  (optional)

Here, fine lamb pieces are tossed in a spicy chili-peanut sauce.
**The result is an addictive, spicy dish that will leave you wanting
more. Perfect served with steamed greens and steamed
jasmine rice.**

Serves 2 cal 412 carbs 10.4g protein 31.4g fat 27.8g

Whisk together all the ingredients for the sauce in a small bowl,
then set aside.

Heat a wok over high heat until smoking and add the canola
oil. When the wok is smoking, add the dried chiles and ground
Sichuan peppercorns and toss for a few seconds. Add the lamb
strips and let sear on one side for 3 seconds, then flip them over.
As the meat starts to turn brown, add the Shaoxing rice wine or
dry sherry.

Give the sauce a stir, then pour into the wok and mix well for
5 seconds. Once the sauce thickens and gives a shine to the
lamb, drizzle with some toasted sesame oil and chili oil and toss
through some dry roasted peanuts and finely chopped cilantro.

Take off the heat and transfer to a serving plate. Serve with
steamed greens and jasmine rice.

20 mins*

5 mins

* includes marinating the beef

DF

Korean Beef Bulgogi Stir-fry

For the marinade
2 garlic cloves, finely grated
2 tablespoons low-sodium light soy sauce
1 teaspoon Korean gochujang chili paste
1 teaspoon rice wine vinegar
½ teaspoon sugar
1 teaspoon pure sesame oil

For the stir-fry
10 ounces sirloin steak, fat trimmed off, sliced against the grain into wafer-thin 2-inch pieces (see Tip)
1 tablespoon canola oil
½ white onion, cut into half-moon slices
1 tablespoon Shaoxing rice wine or dry sherry
1 green bell pepper, seeded and cut into 1-inch chunks
pinch of Korean gochugaru chile pepper flakes
pinch of cracked black pepper
2 scallions, finely sliced on an angle

To serve
toasted white sesame seeds, (optional)
1 cup steamed greens
1½ cups steamed jasmine rice (optional)

I love the flavors of Beef Bulgogi—punchy, savory, and sweet with heady hints of garlic and sesame. In the classic Korean dish, the beef is marinated and cooked on a hot table-top hibachi grill, but I marinate the beef and wok it with onions and green bell peppers. A bit of creative license here by adding the Korean gochujang chili paste—and why not, it's delicious! Perfect served with steamed greens and rice.

Serves 2 cal 323 carbs 8.7g protein 37.9g fat 15.4g

Whisk together all the ingredients for the marinade in a bowl. Pour over the beef slices and let marinate for 10 minutes.

Heat a wok over high heat until smoking, then add the canola oil. Toss in the white onion and stir-fry for 20 seconds until golden and seared at the edges, then add the marinated beef and stir-fry for 5 seconds to sear the edges. Add the Shaoxing rice wine or dry sherry and toss in the green bell pepper pieces. Stir-fry over high heat until all the liquid has evaporated, the green bell peppers are al dente but have softened, and the beef is cooked through but still tender. Season with the gochugaru flakes and black pepper. Take off the heat and stir in the scallions.

Transfer to a serving plate immediately, sprinkle with the toasted sesame seeds (if you like).

CHING'S TIP
For wafer-thin slices, wrap the beef in plastic wrap and freeze until firm (but not rock hard). Once firm, slice the beef thinly across the grain.

DF

Xian Lamb with Stir-fried Potatoes

For the spice paste
¼ teaspoon chili powder
½ teaspoon ground cumin
½ teaspoon ground turmeric
½ teaspoon medium curry
   powder
½ teaspoon fennel seeds

For the stir-fry
9 ounces organic lamb loin,
   sliced into ½-inch strips
4 ounces new potatoes,
   unpeeled
1 tablespoon canola oil
2 small red shallots, finely diced
1 tablespoon Shaoxing rice wine
   or dry sherry
1 teaspoon chili bean paste
½ cup hot vegetable stock
1 tablespoon low-sodium light
   soy sauce
1 tablespoon cornstarch blended
   with 1 tablespoon cold water
1 scallion, finely sliced

This spiced lamb stir-fry with potatoes is a Chinese fusion-style stir-fry recipe inspired by my visit to Xian in 2012. The spices are borrowed from Central China and the chili bean paste from Sichuan (Western China). Delicious with jasmine rice or some flatbread.

Serves 2 cal 337 carbs 22g protein 27.8g fat 16.5g

Combine all the ingredients for the spice paste in a bowl, add the lamb, and turn to coat in the paste. Let marinate for 20 minutes. Meanwhile, boil the potatoes.

Heat a wok over high heat until smoking and add the canola oil. Add the shallots and stir-fry for a few seconds to release their aroma. Add the marinated lamb and let it settle in the wok for 10 seconds, then flip it over and stir-fry for 20 seconds.

Add the Shaoxing rice wine or dry sherry. Add the cooked potatoes and the chili bean paste and stir-fry for a few seconds. Add the stock and season with the light soy sauce. Bring to a simmer, then stir in the blended cornstarch to thicken the sauce. As soon as the sauce bubbles and the ingredients are all coated and warmed through with the sauce, it's ready to serve. Give it one final stir, then garnish with the scallion and serve immediately.

Sichuan Lamb

1 tablespoon canola oil

1 green chile, seeded and finely chopped

1 medium onion, cut into half-moon slices

a large handful of long dried chiles

9 ounces lamb loin, cut into ½-inch x 1-inch length slices

pinch of Chinese five-spice powder

1 tablespoon Shaoxing rice wine or dry sherry

2 celery ribs, sliced diagonally into 1-inch pieces

1 tablespoon chili bean paste

1 tablespoon Chinkiang black rice vinegar or balsamic vinegar

1 tablespoon low-sodium light soy sauce

1 teaspoon chili oil

handful of roasted peanuts

small handful of fresh cilantro stems and leaves, coarsely chopped

Calling all spicy food lovers—this addictive dish is perfect made with beef, lamb, or even tender goat. For my vegan friends, use smoked tofu slices. The onions provide sweetness against the spicy hit of the Sichuan peppercorns, and the celery gives a tasty aniseed flavor and delightful crunchy texture. Serve with steamed jasmine rice.

Serves 2 cal 389 carbs 13.9g protein 31g fat 24.1g

Heat a wok over high heat until smoking and add the canola oil. Add the green chile, onion, and dried chiles and stir-fry for 15 seconds to soften and release their aroma and caramelize at the edges.

Add the lamb loin and leave for 3 seconds, then toss to cook for 30 seconds. Add the five-spice powder and Shaoxing rice wine or dry sherry. Toss in the celery pieces and stir-fry over high heat for 30 seconds. Drizzle a small dash of water around the edge of the wok to create steam to help cook the celery.

Season with the chili bean paste, vinegar, light soy sauce, and chili oil. Add the roasted peanuts and toss all together. Stir in the cilantro and serve immediately.

Glossary

Bamboo shoots
These add a crunchy texture to dishes. Boiled bamboo sprouts are also pickled in brine, giving them a sour taste, and in chili oil, which gives them a spicy taste.

Bok choy
A vegetable with broad green leaves, which taper to white stalks. Crisp and crunchy, it can be boiled, steamed or stir-fried.

Buckwheat Noodles
Made from 100 percent buckwheat flour, they contain nutrients such as protein, complex carbohydrates, and thiamine and manganese. They are also gluten- and fat-free.

Chili bean paste
Made from fava beans and chiles that have been fermented with salt to give a deep brown-red sauce. Some versions include fermented soybeans or garlic. Good in soups and braised dishes, it should be used with caution, as some varieties are extremely hot.

Chili oil
A fiery, orange-red oil made by heating dried red chiles in oil. To make your own, heat peanut oil in a wok, add dried chile flakes with seeds and cook for 2 minutes. Take off the heat and leave the chile to infuse in the oil until completely cooled. Decant into a glass jar and store for a month before using. For a clear oil, pass through a strainer.

Chili sauce/chili garlic sauce
A bright red, hot sauce made from chiles, vinegar, sugar, and salt. Some varieties are flavored with garlic and vinegar.

Chinese celery
Chinese celery stalks are slimmer and more tender than the Western variety and the flavor is more intense. Both the stalks and leaves are used.

Chinese cabbage
This has a delicate, sweet aroma with a mild flavor that disappears when cooked. The white stalk has a crunchy texture and remains succulent even after prolonged cooking. The Koreans mainly use it for kimchi.

Chinese chives (garlic chives)
Long, flat, green leaves with a strong garlic flavor. There are two varieties, one has small yellow flowers at the top, which can be eaten. Both are delicious.

Chinese egg noodles
Made from egg yolk, wheat flour, and salt, and available fresh or dried, these come in a variety of thickness and shapes—flat and thin, long and rounded like spaghetti, and flat and coiled in a ball. If you can't find them, use the wide, flat egg noodles found in supermarkets.

Chinese five-spice powder
A blend of five spices—cinnamon, cloves, Sichuan peppercorns, fennel, and star anise—that give the distinctive sour, bitter, pungent, sweet, and salty flavors of Chinese cooking. This spice works extremely well with meats and in marinades.

Chinese sausages
These vary in fattiness and sugar content. Although most are made from pork, some use a mixture of offal and belly (and are infused with spices and rice wine). Depending on their dryness they may need to be steam-cooked before slicing and adding to stir-fries.

Chinese sesame paste
Made from crushed roasted white sesame seeds blended with toasted sesame oil, it is used with other sauces to flavor dishes. If you cannot find it, you can use tahini instead, but it is a lot lighter in flavor so you will need to add more toasted sesame oil.

Chinese wood ear mushrooms
Dark brown-black fungi with ear-shaped caps. Very crunchy in texture, they do not impart flavor but add crispness. They should be soaked in hot water for 20 minutes before cooking—they will double in size.

Chinkiang black rice vinegar
A strong aromatic vinegar made from fermented rice. The taste is mellow and earthy and it gives dishes a wonderful smoky flavor. Balsamic vinegar makes a good substitute.

Choy sum
A green leafy vegetable with a thick stem and tender leaves that belongs to the Brassica family, it is delicious either steamed or stir-fried. Broccolini is a good substitute.

Cinnamon stick/bark
The dried bark of various trees in the Cinnamomum family. It can be used in pieces or ground. Ground adds a sweet, woody fragrance.

Congee
Plain soupy rice porridge that can be combined with other ingredients, such as salted peanuts, fermented bean curd, and chile-pickled bamboo shoots.

Daikon (white radish)
Resembling a large white carrot, this crunchy vegetable has a peppery taste and pungent smell, and is eaten raw, pickled, or cooked. It contains vitamin C and diastase, which aids digestion. Koreans use it to make kimchi.

Deep-fried dofu
Fresh bean curd that has been deep-fried to a golden brown to make it crispy and crunchy on the outside.

Dofu—see Fresh bean curd

Dried Chinese mushrooms
These need to be soaked in hot water for 20 minutes before cooking. They have a strong aroma and a slightly salty taste and therefore complement savory dishes well.

Dried shrimp
Orange-red and very pungent, these shrimp have been cooked and then dried and salted. To use, soak in hot water for 20 minutes, then drain.

Dried Sichuan chiles/chile flakes
Hot and fragrant, these chiles are usually sun-dried. You can grind the whole chiles in a mortar and pestle to give flakes.

Dried upward heaven-facing chile
Also known as "facing heaven pepper," this medium hot, cone-shaped chile is used dried as it is too hot to be eaten raw. A good substitute is dried cayenne pepper.

Edamame beans
These are harvested while the beans are still attached to the bushy branches on which they grow (*eda* means "branches" and *mame* "beans" in Japanese). High in protein, they are cooked whole and the seeds are then squeezed out.

Enoki mushrooms
Tiny, white, very thin, long-stemmed mushrooms with a delicate flavor. Used raw, they add texture to salads. Lightly steamed, they are slight chewy.

Fermented cucumber kimchi
Known as *oi sobagi*, there are two types: wet and dry. Dry has a crunchy texture, the wet a softer one. If you can't find them, use small cucumbers and quickly "pickle" by adding to fermented kimchi cabbage.

Fermented fish paste
Fish that has been fermented until it has become a salty, smooth paste. A little goes a long way.

Fermented salted black beans
Small black soybeans preserved in salt, which must be rinsed in cold water before use. They are used to make black bean sauce.

Fermented yellow bean paste
Made from yellow soybeans, water, and salt. A cheat substitute would be hoisin sauce, although this is sweeter and not as salty.

Fish sauce
A light amber liquid extracted from fermented fish and sea salt. The first press—made without additives or sugar—is the most prized.

Fresh bean curd (dofu/tofu)
Described as the "cheese" of China, this is made from soybean curd and is quite bland, but takes on the flavor of whatever ingredients it is cooked with. Called tofu in Japan and dofu in Chinese, it is high in protein and also contains B vitamins, isoflavones, and calcium. Available

as firm, soft, and silken, the firm variety is great in soups, salads, and stir-fries. Silken has a cream cheese-like texture. *Dofu gan* is dried firm smoked bean curd.

Gai lan (Chinese broccoli)
Unlike Western green broccoli, *gai lan* comes in several varieties, some with yellow flowers, although most have large, glossy, blue-green leaves with long, thick, crisp chunky stems. A good substitute is broccolini.

Goji berry (Chinese wolfberry)
The deep red, dried fruit of an evergreen shrub. Similar to a raisin, it is sweet and nutritionally rich, and can be eaten raw or cooked.

Hoisin sauce
Made from fermented soybeans, sugar, vinegar, star anise, sesame oil, and red rice, this is great used as a marinade and as a dipping sauce.

Jasmine rice
A long-grain white rice originating from Thailand that has a nutty jasmine-scented aroma. You need to rinse it before cooking until the water runs clear to get rid of any excess starch.

Jicama (Mexican yam bean/turnip)
Called *dòush* in China, this is papery yellow on the outside with a creamy white crisp texture inside resembling pear or raw potato. Sweet and starchy in taste, it pairs well with lemon or lime juice. Use crisp Asian pear or pear as a substitute.

Kaffir lime leaves
The leaves of the citrus fruit native to tropical Asia. The leaves emit an intense citrus aroma. Try sourcing online if unavailable in Asian grocery stores.

Kimchi
A Korean staple made from salted and fermented Chinese cabbage mixed with Korean radish, Korean dried chile flakes, scallions, ginger, and *geotgal* (salted seafood).

Korean chile flakes (gochugaru)
Made by first drying the chiles in the sun, then seeding and crushing them, these vibrant red flakes impart a spicy taste with a hint of sweetness. A good substitute is dried chile flakes.

Korean chili paste (gochujang)
A savory, sweet, fermented paste made from Korean red chili powder, glutinous rice, and salt-and-barley malt powder. Soybeans are also sometimes used.

Korean yellow bean paste
Similar to Chinese yellow bean paste and Japanese miso, this made from fermented soybeans and brine. It is also flavored with garlic and sesame oil and mixed with Korean chili paste to produce *samjang*, a sauce that accompanies meat dishes.

Lemongrass (citronella root)
A tough, lemon-scented stalk popular in Thai and Vietnamese cuisines. Look for lemon-green stalks that are tightly formed, firm, and heavy with no bruising, tapering to a deeper green toward the end.

Mock duck
A vegetarian ingredient made from wheat gluten, soy, sugar, salt, and oil. A good substitute is bean curd or tofu skin.

Mirin
A sweet Japanese rice wine similar to sake, with a lower alcohol content but a higher sugar one (the sugar occurs naturally as a result of the fermentation process).

Miso paste
A thick Japanese paste made from fermented rice, barley, soybeans, salt, and a fungus called *kojikin*. Sweet, earthy, fruity, and salty, it comes in many varieties depending on the types of grains used.

Mung bean noodles
Made from the starch of green mung beans and water, these noodles come in various thicknesses, vermicelli being the thinnest. To use, soak in hot water for 5 to 6 minutes before cooking. If using in soups or deep-frying, no presoaking is necessary. They become translucent when cooked.

Mushroom oyster sauce—see Oyster sauce

Nori (dried seaweed)
Sold in thin sheets, this is usually roasted over a flame until it turns black or purple-green. Used as a garnish or to wrap sushi, once opened, a pack must be sealed and stored in an airtight container or it loses its crispness. If this happens, just roast the sheets over an open flame for a few seconds until crisp.

Oyster mushrooms
Soft and chewy with a slight oyster taste, this white, yellow, or gray oyster-shaped fungi is moist and fragrant.

Oyster sauce
A seasoning sauce made from oyster extract that can also be used as a marinade. A vegetarian variety is also available. It is very salty, so taste the dish before adding.

Pad Thai noodles
Flat noodles, ¼-inch wide, made from rice. They need to be soaked in hot water for 5 minutes before cooking.

Panko bread crumbs
Made from bread without crusts, these Japanese bread crumbs have a crisp texture.

Persian cucumbers
Small, thin-skinned cucumbers, 4 to 6 inches long, with soft, tiny seeds, Mild and sweet.

Potato flour
A smooth, gluten-free flour made from potatoes that are steamed, dried, and then ground. It gives wonderful crispness when used to coat ingredients before frying.

Ramen
Noodles, invented in China, that are used in Japanese noodle soups. They come in various thicknesses and shapes, but most are made from wheat flour, salt, water, and *kansui* (alkaline mineral water), the latter ingredient gives the noodles a yellow hue and a firmer texture.

Red miso paste—see Miso paste

Rice vinegar
A clear (white), mild vinegar made from fermented rice. Cider vinegar can be used as a substitute. Chinese black rice vinegar is a rich, aromatic vinegar that is used in braised dishes and sauces, and with noodles. When cooked, it gives a smoky flavor with a mellow and earthy taste. Balsamic vinegar makes a good substitute.

Sake
A fermented Japanese drink made from polished rice brewed in a similar way to wine. Alcohol content ranges from 15 to 20 percent.

Sambal oelek
A staple in Malaysian and Thai cooking used to add heat to dishes. Made from fiery red chiles, vinegar, and salt. A little goes a long way.

Sesame seeds
These oil-rich seeds add a nutty taste and a delicate texture to many Asian dishes. Available in black, white/yellow, and red varieties, toasted and untoasted.

Shaoxing rice wine
Made from rice, millet, and yeast aged for 3 to 5 years, it takes the "odor" or "rawness" from meats and fish and gives a bittersweet finish. Dry sherry makes a good substitute.

Shiitake mushrooms
These large, nutrient-rich, dark brown umbrella-shaped fungi are prized for their culinary and medicinal properties. The dried variety needs to be soaked in water for 20 minutes before cooking.

Shimeji (beech) mushrooms
These come in white or brown varieties, and are characterized by long stems and tight concave caps. They are sold at most farmer's markets. If you can't find them, use another mushroom of your choice.

Shichimi pepper flakes/Japanese chile flakes (nana-iro togarashi)
A Japanese spice that contains roasted orange peel, white and black sesame seeds, hemp seeds, nori, and ground ginger, red chile pepper, and Sichuan peppercorns.

Shishito peppers
Small, finger-long, thin-skinned sweet Asian peppers that turn from green to red, although they are usually harvested while still green. The tip is also known as *shizi* (lion in Mandarin), hence its name. Before cooking, you need to poke with a hole to prevent hot air from building up inside and bursting the chile.

Shrimp paste
A dry, smooth paste made by adding salt to shrimp or fish broth, this is then stored overnight, drained, and sun-dried. The mixture is then ground and left to ferment in an earthenware jar. A good paste should be dark deep purple.

Sichuan peppercorns
Known as "Hua jiao" in Mandarin or "flower pepper," these have a pungent, citrusy aroma. They can be wok-roasted, used to flavor oil, or mixed with salt as a condiment.

Somen noodles
Very fine, dried wheat flour noodles, also known as "longevity" noodles, and traditionally eaten on festivals and birthdays.

Soy sauce
Made from wheat and fermented soybeans, soy sauce is available in dark and light varieties. Dark soy sauce is aged a lot longer than the light variety, and is mellower and less salty. Light soy sauce is used in China instead of salt. Wheat-free varieties, called tamari, are available, although it is quite salty. You can also buy low-sodium varieties.

Soybean noodles
Thin, gluten-free dried noodles that are rich in protein, and low in fat. They yield about double the amount of wheat flour noodles once rehydrated.

Sriracha chili sauce
A hot sauce made from chile peppers, distilled vinegar, garlic, salt, and sugar. It is named after the coastal town of Si Racha, Eastern Thailand.

Star anise
The fruit of a small evergreen plant, these are called *bajio* or "eight horns" in Chinese. They have a distinct aniseed flavor and are one of the ingredients found in Chinese five-spice powder.

Taiwanese nine-pagoda leaf basil
This herb has a clove, lemon. and licorice scent. Use Thai sweet basil as a substitute.

Tamari—see Soy sauce

Thai eggplant
Thai varieties are smaller than Western eggplants (often no bigger than a golf ball), and are usually green and white. The smallest are known as pea eggplant, the long, thin purple varieties as Asian eggplant.

Tian mian jiang (sweet bean sauce)
A thick, smooth, opaque dark brown sauce made from wheat flour, salt, sugar, and fermented yellow soybeans. Hoisin is sometimes used as an alternative, although it is much sweeter.

Toasted sesame oil
Made from white pressed and toasted sesame seeds, this oil is used as a flavoring/seasoning and is not suitable for use as a cooking oil since it burns easily. The flavor is intense, so use sparingly.

Tofu—see Fresh bean curd

Vermicelli mung bean noodles—see Mung bean noodles

Vermicelli rice noodle
Similar to vermicelli mung bean noodles, they come in many different widths and varieties. Before cooking, soak in hot water for 5 minutes. If using in salads, soak for 20 minutes. If using in a soup, add them dry.

Water chestnuts
The roots of an aquatic plant that grows in freshwater ponds, marshes, and lakes, and in slow-moving rivers and streams. Unpeeled, they resemble a chestnut in shape and coloring. They have a firm, crunchy texture.

Wheat flour noodles
Thin, white dried noodles. Do not confuse these with thick Japanese udon noodles.

Yellow bean sauce
Made from fermented yellow soybeans, dark brown sugar, and rice wine, this is a very popular flavoring ingredient in Sichuan and Hunan province in China. It also makes a great marinade for meats. Yellow bean paste is a thicker consistency and is used in marinades and as a flavoring in many savory dishes.

Zha cai (Sichuan vegetable)
A popular Sichuan pickled mustard vegetable used in hot and sour soups and dan dan noodles. The knobbly fist-sized stems are salted, pressed, dried, and then covered in hot chili paste and fermented in an earthenware jar (similar to that of Korean kimchi). The taste is spicy, salty, and sour with a crunchy texture. Excess salt can be removed by soaking in fresh water. Usually sold in vacuum packs either whole or presliced.

Index

Acknowledgments

I owe a big thank you to Kyle Cathie and my editor, Judith Hannam. Writing a book can be a scary process, sometimes full of self-doubt, but I am truly blessed to have your belief and support of my work.

This book could not have happened without my literary agent, Heather Holden Brown, who helped make it a reality. Thank you, also, to Toby Eady and Xinran Xue for being my cheerleaders and always guiding me.

A huge thanks to all my fans for continuing to support me on my culinary journey—this book is for you. I have tried to incorporate as many vegan and vegetarian recipes as possible, as this is something I am often asked, and half the book is veggie friendly. I hope you enjoy the recipes as much as I have enjoyed creating them for you. I am indebted and ever grateful for your love.

I am extremely honored to have the friendship of chef Tom Kerridge. I adore, admire, and respect your work greatly. It means so much to me to have your support.

The talented team at Kyle Books are just incredible—xie xie to Editorial Assistant Hannah Coughlin and my copy editor Barbara Dixon (who I have had the pleasure of working with for many years now), for your amazing attention to detail. Thank you to Caroline Clark for the funky design of the book. I raise more than a glass to the incredible Tamin Jones for the photography, to the talented Aya Nishimura for the beautiful food styling, and of course the one and only Wei Tang for the props, as well as special thanks to Nic Jones and Gemma John for the production of the book.

My agent and friend, Kate Heather, you have championed me and continue to support me through thick and thin, helping me so much while juggling babies and family life. Thank you for all your hard work and belief from your no.1 daughter.

Thank you to Michael Kagan at ICM Talent and assistant Colin Burke in the US for continuing to support my career and for believing in me.

Thanks to all the powers at BBC, ITV, Food Network UK and US, the Cooking Channel, and NBC for continuing to give me opportunities and allowing me to share my cooking on TV.

To all my family near or far, especially my mum and dad, it has not always been a "lovely" life for us. I wouldn't be here without you and I am so proud of how far we have come as a family. This book is also for my three grandmas—Wu, Huang, and Carmel Longhurst—you are my angels, looking out for me, giving me love, strength, and inspiration.

To Jamie, my husband, I drive you crazy with my Stir Crazy. Thank you for putting up with everything I dish out—you are my everything.